Holy Spirit
Manufactured Prayer

856-283-8132

The Holy Spirit is a Person. He is the only truthful friend you will
ever need. Friendship with Him means communion, direction,
intimacy and depth, in the things of God.

Yahweh Bless you

5/24/13

Holy Spirit Manufactured Prayer

Learn to Activate Angels of the LORD by
Engaging in Kingdom Principles
Through Prayer

Matthew Dare O'Dunlami

Holy Spirit Manufactured Prayer
Learn to Activate Angels of The LORD by Engaging in
Kingdom Principles Through Prayer
by Matthew Dare O'Dunlami

Printed in the United States of America

ISBN 9781591609247

Please take note that the name satan and other related names are not capitalized. This is intentional so as not to give him the honor of capitalizing his names, even to the point of violating grammatical rules.

Contact:
Matthew O'Dunlami
P. O. Box 567
Sicklerville, NJ 08081
Email: hsmanufacturedprayer@gmail.com

www.xulonpress.com

DEDICATION

To the LORD JESUS CHRIST

My heavenly Father

My tireless Intercessor

My great Teacher

My loyal Advocate

My inconceivable Comforter

My living Word

My faithful Shepherd

My sovereign Savior

My incredible Master

My beloved Friend

My majestic King

My life Giver

My High Priest

My Alpha and Omega.

I also want to gratefully acknowledge through this book my parents, Emmanuel S. O'Dunlami and Comfort Lola O'Dunlami, who are both now with the Lord. My parents each contributed immeasurably to my spiritual growth.

TABLE OF CONTENTS

FOREWORD

Watch therefore, and <u>pray always</u>, that you may be accounted worthy to escape all these things that will come to pass, and to stand before the Son of Man. (Luke 21:36)

But you, beloved, building yourselves up on your most holy faith, <u>praying in the Holy Ghost.</u> (Jude 20)

Praying always and praying in the Holy Ghost are two of the most essential traits a God-fearing Christian can possess. Praying always denotes a mindset of an individual who enjoys living in the presence of God. Someone who recognizes that it's in Him we live, and move and have our very being and it's by Him that all things exist! That individual recognizes that He's like liquid fire, consuming everything in its midst with amazing power and glory.

I will never forget the first time I laid eyes on this anointed man, who walked into our church service one Sunday morning. We were worshipping in this small hotel room, down the hall and around the corner from the main lobby. He came in from the rear entrance of the church room and walked down the center aisle. He passed by everyone and stopped on the front row and sat next to me, not knowing that I was the pastor. I introduced myself to him, he was kind and very cordial, however, there was fire in his eyes. I ministered the word of God that Sunday and as I was ending service, the Holy Ghost said, "Give him space to speak". I yielded to the Holy Ghost and for the next thirty minutes, Prophet Matthew spoke the word of God with fire and conviction. He prayed, prophesied and spoke the word of God over our ministry, our natural family and church family with boldness.

Romans 8:26b states, "......*but the Spirit itself makes intercession for us with groanings which cannot be uttered.*" However, **Holy Spirit Manufactured Prayer** goes far beyond just asking God for the temporal things of this world that will soon vanish away. It's dives into the spiritual realm of man, "*for the word of God is living and powerful, and sharper than any two-edged sword piercing even to the division of soul and spirit, and its joints and marrow, and is a discerner of the thoughts and intents of the heart*". (Hebrews 4:12)

A daily devotional with your heavenly Father is essential! Seeking His face and knowing His desires and choices for your life will prepare you to stand before the Son of man. Prophet Matthew exhibits the qualities of a spiritual leader who can help increase your relationship with your heavenly Father! We both agree that it takes perseverance, desire and determination to hear the will of God, follow His directions and speak His word with boldness. Pray always and do not faint!

Rodney Sanders, Senior Pastor
The Voice of One Ministry

****

INTRODUCTION

God inspired me to write this prayer book, *Holy Spirit Manufactured Prayer,* for members of the body of Christ who have a great desire to pray and who are willing to stand in all their heavenly requests, until they receive complete manifestation and answers to their prayers. The purpose of this prayer book is also to encourage the Body of Christ to engage in vigorous prayer until Christ comes, enhancing and enlarging your personal relationship with Jesus. As a result, you will begin to intercede for your family, souls, leaders in government, your community, believers and non-believers around the globe. (Esther 4:14-17) Every believer needs to obey Him and since we carry His zeal of the Holy Spirit inside us, His power in our prayers will anoint, inspire and direct us to fulfill our destiny, as God ordained for our lives. *"If My people who are called by My name will humble themselves, and pray and seek My face, and turn from their wicked ways,*

then I will hear from heaven, and will forgive their sin and heal their land." (2 Chronicles 7:14)

The more you engage in the lifestyle of an intercessor, you will begin to see signs and wonders. Speaking the Word of God loudly in prayer, releases power into the atmosphere of your situation and this will change things more quickly for you. *"Death and life are in the power of the tongue, And those who love it will eat its fruit."* (Proverbs 18:21)

Prayer will also change your personal revelation, visions and dreams. There is no limit to open heavens and to your breakthrough in spiritual realms. Our Lord Jesus Christ is our true Intercessor and the Holy Spirit is there for us to guide, lead, teach and inform us of all we need to know. Heaven will open to you, providing all the help you need to live success-fully here on earth, in Jesus' Name.

This is a daily devotional and every single prayer has been inspired through a divine encounter with the Holy Spirit, including revelations, visions, and dreams, confirmed by Scriptures.

Holy Spirit manufactures prayer for us because He knows the mind of God. Throughout Scripture when God spoke, it was creative and always revealed something about *Himself, His purposes, or His ways*. I believe the true purpose of God in revealing the future and giving instruction in dreams and visions involves four aspects of our walk with God. The four aspects found in the book of Genesis, chapter 22, where God revealed to Abraham *His plan, His place, His provision,* and *His purpose* for his life. God's revelations are designed to bring us into a love relationship with Him.

"However, when He, the Spirit of truth, has come, He will guide you into all truth; for He will not speak on His own authority; but whatever He hears He will speak; and He will tell you things to come. He will glorify Me, for He will take of what is Mine and declare it to you. All things that the Father has are Mine. Therefore I said that He will take of Mine and declare it to you." (John 16:13-15)

There are three different levels of "sights" to develop simultaneously while using this prayer book; Holy Spirit manufactured prayer which can only be accomplished through the power of the Holy Spirit.

"And Elisha prayed, and said 'LORD, I pray, open his eyes that he may see.' Then the LORD opened the eyes of the young man, and he saw. And behold, the mountain was full of horses and chariots of fire all around Elisha." (2 Kings 6:17)

Physical sight or natural sight:

"Watch and pray, lest you enter into temptation. The spirit indeed is willing, but the flesh is weak." (Matthew 26:41) Often, while we are praying, ours eyes are wandering and brings unwanted distraction.

Mental sight or scriptural sight:

"But even if our gospel is veiled, it is veiled to those who are perishing, Whose minds the god of this age has blinded, who do not believe, lest the light of the gospel of the glory of Christ, who is the image of God, should shine on them." (2 Corinthians 4:3-4). We need to develop a lifestyle of reading the bible daily and pray for understanding of what the Scriptures are saying to us, each and every day!

Spiritual sight or revelations, dreams and visions

The ability to see things from the spiritual realm before it happens is paramount to our spiritual growth and our destiny. Fellowship with our Lord Jesus Christ, through prayer, helps to see the invisible, to hear the inaudible, and to speak like an oracle of God.

For example, let us examine how Jesus Himself revealed and demonstrated the importance of these three types of sight, to the two disciples, on the road to Emmaus. When Jesus was talking to them, the bible says, *"their eyes were restrained so they did not know Him"*, (Luke 24:16) which is their physical or natural sight.

Then He said to them *"O foolish ones, and slow of heart to believe in all that the prophets have spoken! "Ought not the Christ to have suffered these things and to enter into His Glory?" And beginning at Moses and all the Prophets, He expounded to them in all the Scriptures the things concerning Himself.* (Luke 24:25-27) This is mental and scriptural sight because Jesus taught them and explained the Scriptures to them. He fed them mentally and He agreed to stay with them and still they did not know who actually was talking to them, because their eyes were still restrained.

"Now it came to pass as He sat at the table with them, that He took bread, blessed and broke it and gave it to them. Then their eyes were opened and they knew Him and He vanished from their sight." We see here the spiritual sight, of these two disciples, were suddenly opened and they were able to see Jesus. We see in the Scripture, when the disciples asked Jesus to teach them how to pray, Jesus responded by giving them what is now called the "Lord's Prayer."

"Our Father in heaven, hallowed be Your name. Your kingdom come. Your will be done on earth as it is in heaven. Give us this day our daily bread and forgive us

our debts, as we forgive our debtors. And do not lead us into temptation but deliver us from the evil one. For Yours is the kingdom and the power and the glory for-ever. Amen." (Matthew 6: 9-13)

This book will change the mind-set from earthly prayers to heavenly prayers. By praying these prayers, your prayer life will change completely:

LORD, open my eyes to see God.

LORD, open my eyes to see myself as You see me from Your throne.

LORD, open my eyes to see my enemies and people around me.

LORD open my eyes to see where I am now; my situation.

LORD, open my eyes to see where I am going, in my life.

When God opens your eyes to see yourself, God, the enemy, where you are and where you are going, you will also experience the anointing power of God as to how to pray and proceed in God's will for your life. *"He reveals deep and secret things; He knows what is in the darkness and light dwells with Him."* (Daniel 2:22)

Holy Spirit Manufactured Prayer book took many years to come into existence. I pray this book will bring the light of God to your life and change your prayer life. Change that is enhanced by the mindset of heaven, as you become more familiar with God's Word and His power, in prayer.

"He shall call upon Me, and I will answer him; I will be with him in trouble; *I will deliver him and honor him. With long life I will satisfy him, And show him My Salvation*". (Psalms 91:15-16)

****

RELATIONSHIP WITH THE LORD JESUS CHRIST
(It is a Prerequisite)

In writing this prayer book, I have assumed that you have already believed and trusted in our Lord Jesus Christ as Savior and you acknowledged Him to be Lord of your life. If you have not made this most important decision in your life, the rest of this prayer book will have little meaning for you because spiritual matters can only be understood by those who have the indwelling Spirit of Christ. *"The natural man does not receive the things of the Spirit of God, for they are foolishness to him; nor can he know them, because they are spiritually discerned."* (1 Corinthians 2:14)

If you sense a need to accept Jesus as your Savior and Lord, now is a good time for you to settle this matter first with God, before you start praying these Holy Spirit inspired prayers. Ask God to speak to you as you read the following Scriptures:

- Read Romans 3:23; All have sinned.
- Read Romans 6:23; Eternal life is a free gift of God.
- Read Romans 5:8; Because of love, Jesus paid the death penalty for your sins.
- Read Romans 10:9; Confess Jesus as Lord and Believe God raised Him from the dead.
- Read Romans 10:13; Ask God to save you and He will.

To place your faith in Christ Jesus and receive His gift of eternal life today, you must:

- Recognize that God created you for a love relationship with Him. He wants you to love Him with all your being.
- Recognize that you are a sinner and you cannot save yourself.
- Believe that Jesus paid a death penalty for your sin by His death on the cross and rose from the dead, in victory over death.
- Confess (agree with God about) your sins that separate you from Him.
- Repent of your sins (turn from sin to God).
- Ask Jesus to save you by His grace (undeserved favor).
- Turn over the rule of your life to Jesus. Let Him be your Lord.

Jesus, come into my life. Forgive me of all my sins. I ask You to cleanse my heart, and make me a new person in You right now. I believe that You are the Son of God and that You died on the cross for me. Jesus I want to thank You for loving me enough to die for me. I accept all that Your shed blood bought for me on the cross, and I receive You as my Savior and Lord. In Your name I pray. Amen.

If you just prayed this prayer, congratulations! You are a "new creature" in Christ Jesus. (2 Corinthians 5:17)

If you need help in making this important decision in your life, call on your pastor, a deacon, an elder or other Christian friend for help. Otherwise, If you have just made this important decision, call someone and share the good news of what God has done in your life. Then share your decision with your church. After you have made this important decision in your life, I know your prayer life cannot be the same again and answers to your prayers can no longer be delayed. We encourage you to make daily **declarations** and **confessions** upon yourself and your family.

The Word of God is Power, when you call upon Him. Let the enemy know you are now a new creation in the Lord Jesus Christ by making true confessions to your life daily. When challenges come your way to discourage you, from your decisions in life, pronounce these confessions daily about your new relationship with the Lord Jesus Christ. "'*I know who I am*" in Christ Jesus.'

I KNOW WHO I AM

- I am born again. (John 3:7)
- I am justified. (Romans 5:1)
- I am Christ's friend. (John 15:15)
- I am God's child. (John 1:12, 4:24)
- I am God's temple. (1 Corinthians 3: 16)
- I am complete in Christ. (Colossians 2: 10)
- I am God's workmanship. (Ephesians 2:10)
- I am a personal witness for Christ. (Acts 1:8)
- I am rise up and call blessed. (Proverb 31:28)
- I am united with the Lord. (1 Corinthians 6:17)
- I am a saint, set apart for God. (Ephesians 1:1)
- I am hidden with Christ in God. (Colossians 3:3)
- I am bought with a price. (1 Corinthians 6:19-20)
- I am the temple of the Holy Spirit. (John 16: 13-15)
- I am the salt & light of the earth. (Matthew 5:13-14)
- I have been adopted as God's child. (Ephesians 1:5)
- I am who live by faith not by sight. (2 Corinthians 5:7)
- I am given a new heart. (Ezekiel 26:26; Jeremiah17:9)
- I have been redeemed and forgiven. (Philippians 1:14)
- I am free forever from condemnation. (Romans 8: 1-2)

- I am justified and made upright by faith. (Romans 3:28)
- I am clothed with the righteousness of God. (Job 29:14)
- I am free from any charge against me. (Romans 8:31-34)
- I am a just person. I shall live by my faith. (Habakkuk 2:4)
- I am a member of the body of Christ. (1 Corinthians 12:27)
- I am a citizen of Heaven. I am significant. (Philippians 3:20)
- I am God's co-worker. (1 Corinthians 3:9; 2 Corinthian 6:1)
- I have been chosen and appointed to bear fruit. (John 15:16)
- I cannot be separated from the love of God. (Romans 8:35-39)
- I am not unequally yoked with unbelievers. (2 Corinthians 6:14)
- I am seated with Christ in the heavenly realms. (Ephesians 2:6)
- I have access to God through the Holy Spirit. (Ephesians 2:18)
- I am assured all things work together for good. (Romans 8: 28)
- I am a minister of reconciliation for God. (2 Corinthians 5:17-21)

- As for me and my house, we will serve the LORD. (Joshua 24:15)
- I am standing firm, letting nothing move me. (1 Corinthians 15:18)
- I am established, anointed, sealed by God. (2 Corinthians 1:21-22)
- I am the branch of the true vine, a channel of His life. (John 15: 1-5)
- I may approach God with freedom and confidence. (Ephesians 3: 12)
- I can do all things through Christ who strengthens me. (Philippians 4:13)
- I am confident that the good works God has begun in me will be perfected. (Philippians 1: 5)

HOW TO USE THIS BOOK
Holy Spirit Manufactured Prayer

P rayer is a special gift and privilege to all mankind. Those who use this gift to its full advantage become the wielders of great authority and power. Even though this great power is available to those who believe, however, we see the average believer does not exercise their supernatural gift. Jesus said, *"And from the days of John the Baptist until now the kingdom of heaven suffers violence, and the violent take it by force."* (Matthew 11:12) Engaging in prayer *(spiritual warfare)* determines your closeness to our Lord Jesus Christ. Jesus said, *"Do not think that I came to bring peace on earth, I did not come to bring peace but a sword."* (*Matthew* 10:34) We enjoy a brighter future as we strengthen our relationship with Christ. The earlier we learn the art of spiritual warfare through dynamic prayer, the better.

Paul wrote in the book of Acts, *"For I know this, that after my departure savage wolves will come in among you, not sparing flock."* (Acts 20:29) Jesus also sent forth seventy appointees and said to them; "'*Go your way; behold, I send you out as lambs among wolves*.'" (Luke 10:3)

Today, if we examine the temperature level of most Christians regarding prayer, we find it needs to be adjusted to a higher level, if they expect serious results.

There are over 1,000 prayer points in this daily devotional book intended to target to all possible areas of life and will change the way you pray forever. Please take note of the following.

You can use the daily devotional in these ways:
- ❖ Praying daily according to the prayers outlined.
- ❖ Privately praying as an individual.
- ❖ During your family's daily devotion time.
- ❖ In a small group fellowship, praying and proclaiming together.
- ❖ In a large group fellowship, praying and proclaiming together.
- ❖ During your Church intercessory prayer meetings.

Though, it is a daily devotional, you can also use while you are in a special time of consecration (incubation) with the Lord. "*And you shall not go outside the door of the tabernacle of meeting for seven days, until the days of your consecra-*

tion are ended. For seven days he shall consecrate you." (Leviticus 8: 33) Prayer is significant while you are in a period of consecration.

❖ Read and meditate on the Scriptures and prayers, and let them all sink into your spirit. (Romans 8:26)

❖ Consecrate one day each week and or month to fast and pray regularly. This discipline helps build a solid relationship with our Lord Jesus Christ. (*Do not fast if you are on medication or are pregnant.*)

❖ Loudly proclaim the prayers, declarations and confessions for the day.

❖ Pray aggressively.

The purpose of **Holy Spirit Manufactured Prayer** is to encourage the Body of Christ to engage in vigorous prayer until Christ returns. *"Even them I will bring to My Holy Mountain, and make them joyful in My house of prayer. Their burnt offerings and their sacrifices will be accepted on My altar; for My house shall be called a house of prayer for all nations."* (Isaiah 56:7)

Requirements before engaging in Spiritual Warfare:

❖ **Adequate preparation is significant.** In most cases we must get our house (mind) in order.

❖ **Spiritual warfare must have a purpose**. Do not fight purposeless wars. Identify the area in which you need to pray aggressively; such as marriage, ministry, finance, family and career.

❖ **Examine yourself thoroughly.** Examine yourself thoroughly making sure there are no loopholes that enemies will capitalize to use or accuse you.

❖ **Have stubborn faith**. You must possess stubborn faith. The blind Bartimaeus kind of faith or faith of the woman with the issue of blood, are significant and powerful. This kind of faith does not give up until there is actual manifestation to prayer.

❖ **Live Holy**. Any form of unrighteousness will render a person powerless and therefore it is necessary to live a lifestyle of holiness.

❖ **Receive adequate instruction**. Using this prayer book will help with proper training and instruction on prayer.

Strategies of Spiritual Warfare:

❖ Determine clearly what you are fighting against.

❖ Declare war against the situation with the Word of God, *prayer, fasting* and a *holy lifestyle*.(Matthew 17:21)

❖ Do not fast if you are on medication or are pregnant.

❖ Pray in the Holy Ghost, (speaking in tongues), at least 30 minutes each day and increase as God gives you utterance. (Jude 1:20)

❖ Fear must be totally erased. (2 Timothy 1:7)

❖ Show **generosity** to those who are in need. (Isaiah 58:7-14)

❖ Show the **love of Christ** to all people. (Ephesians 3:19)

❖ Persistently proclaim the Blood of Jesus and apply it to all situations in life. (Hebrews 10:19)

❖ Remember, victory is yours…permanently!

ENCOURAGEMENT

G od is working more exceedingly in our world today than ever before in history to draw all people to Himself through prayer. He is working to purify His people and nations, in order to exalt His Son Jesus Christ. He is breaking down barriers to the gospel message and is calling people to intercessory service in unprecedented numbers. He is raising up godly leaders and ministries to speak to His people and to a lost world. God is marshalling His forces for a tremendous work of grace in our lifetime!

I pray that God will use this prayer book, *Holy Spirit Manufactured Prayer*, to radically touch your life for the expansion of His kingdom. His work in your life will far surpass all your plans and dreams and the glory of the Lord shall be revealed, while all flesh will see it together, in Jesus' Name. He will bring purpose and fulfillment to your life and ministry with unspeakable and overflowing joy. In days ahead, He will be calling you to join Him as an intercessory-ally to reach our world. I pray that you will be very responsive to Him in the coming days, as you use this prayer book daily.

Your assigned angels from the throne of our Father in heaven may have never been activated or employed to ministering salvation and strength to you. Remember angels only harken to the Word of God spoken through your intercessory prayers.

The LORD has established His throne in heaven, And His kingdom rules over all. *"Bless the LORD you His angels, Who excel, in strength, who do His Word, Heeding the voice of His Word." (*Psalms 103:19-20, Hebrew 1:14*)*

Now it is time for you to start engaging these angels of God by speaking the Word of God to the atmosphere of your situations. *"But when He again brings the firstborn into the world, He says, Let all the angels of God worship Him. And of the angels He says, Who makes His angels spirits and His ministers a flame of fire."* (Hebrew 1:6-7)

John said, *"And I fell at his feet to worship him. But he said to me, 'See that you do not do that! I am your fellow servant, and of your brethren who have the testimony of Jesus. Worship God! For the testimony of Jesus is the spirit of prophecy.'"* (Revelation 19:10)

May the grace, joy, and peace of God be yours through Jesus Christ, our Living Lord, to Him be the glory, now and forever. Shalom, Shalom!!

TESTIMONIALS

I have compiled few testimonies from our brothers and sisters just like you to encourage you as you use your daily devotional guidance with the Lord book. I pray that as they had experienced with these prayers, you too will have the same encounter with the Holy Ghost. I believe your testimonies are waiting for you. Today, the angels of LORD are quietly waiting for your prayers to be delivered from the throne of Almighty God. Please read these testimonies and believe you will receive answers to ALL your prayers. The testimony of Jesus is the spirit of prophecy. (Revelation 19:10)

Testimonial-1

Arthur Anderson; III, Broomall, PA

In January 2004, Matthew O'Dunlami told me, it was time to move my family from the Overbrook section of Philadelphia. Deep in my heart, I was not ready to move, as things were very comfortable for me and my wife. We both worked but we were able to live primarily off my salary and save a good portion of hers. However, I submitted to the Lord and began searching for a new home in Delaware County. In March, we found a house that we both liked but it was significantly more than what we wanted to spend. We made several offers that were lower than the asking price, but each time the buyers declined our offer. One Saturday afternoon I invited Matthew to see the house and to pray. When we got to the house, he asked me if I liked the house and I replied yes. He then told me to go ahead and use the bathroom, yet I told him I did not have to go. Eventually, I yielded to his instructions and when I came back out, he told me I will use this bathroom all the time. I just laughed. Finally, we prayed and asked God to work everything out, including, the proper mortgage to purchase our new home and finding a buyer for our existing home that could close in 45 days. We left the house that day.

In April, God answered our prayers and the closing dates for both transactions were scheduled on the same day, May 7th 2004. On closing day, I received a phone call from my realtor notifying me that my buyer was unable to close. I was devastated, as the close for the new home was contingent upon us being able to successfully close on our existing home. But then a voice spoke to me and instructed me to call my bank and explain the situation. I'm here to tell you, God worked out this situation as well. We were able to close on the new home and within two weeks we closed on our existing home. God is good!!

After being in our new home for almost a year, I was unexpectedly laid off from work. Although I experienced God's deliverance and divine intervention on several other issues, that was not on the forefront of my mind. I immediately went into seeking God's face. After spending two weeks in my cave trying to work things out on my own, several thought provoking questions went through my mind. Did not God tell me to move? Did not God work out everything for me to be here? Did not God provide a job for me before? I soon realized that once again God was testing my faith. I concluded that God would sustain me and my family and He would provide the right job in His own time. One Sunday afternoon, Matthew came to visit, not knowing I was laid off. Apparently God had instructed him to visit me and my family that day. Well, we talked and I shared with him what I was going through. We immediately began to pray and ask God for His help. The following Monday morning, I received a phone call about a job opportunity with an inner city Hospital asking me to start work the next day as a consultant. Six years later I'm still employed by the same Hospital, where God has allowed me to find favor. Thank you Father for keeping me and my family!!! . I thank God for this man of God.

****

Testimonial-2

Abiola Saba; Sewell, NJ

In December 2007, on a Sunday morning, I realized something was not right with my son. I called my husband and we took him to the emergency room. By the time we got to the Emergency room, things had changed. The emergency team took him from us, and the running began. We were told our son was in a coma and needed to be transferred to the critical care unit, where the neurologist and his team, were waiting. "Are you kidding me," I kept asking? "This cannot be true," I told my husband. "I must be dreaming," I said. "Please, tell me I am dreaming," I said crying. When we got to the critical care unit, I could not recognize my son, with all the tubing and IV's connected to him. Like any caring parent, I was devastated. It was around Christmas, with everyone in a festive mood. Still lost in my thoughts, when a doctor introduced himself as my son's pediatrician, I was happy that this doctor will be able to answer all my questions. A few minutes into our conversation, I realized my spirit was rejecting what this doctor was sharing and as he was saying things contrary to what I believed in. He was making a prediction that I refused to receive, as a child of God.

After all the commotion, I settled in my son's hospital room, not knowing what to do. Prayer I know is an option, but at that moment I was very emotional and drowning in self pity.

Eventually, I snapped out of my pity party realizing I was the only guest and no one was interested in attending it with me. I prayed and at the end of my prayers, I decided to call Pastor Matthew. A few minutes later my phone rang and as a result of the distraction, I forget to call Pastor Matthew.

By day five of my son being in a coma, and trying to hold on to what was left of my faith, I called Brother Matthew. He was at work, but told me he will come see me. A few hours later, he arrived and I jumped in excitement. I just knew within me that The Lord would do something through His anointed servant. Pastor Mathew said God had given him some instructions. I noticed that he did not get close to my son. Yet later, he approached him and held my son in his right hand and asked me to hold him on the other side of the bed. My faith was strong that something unique and supernatural was going to happen. My husband, my Pastor, Pastor Matthew and I, were all in the intensive care unit with my son. Pastor Matthew shared some instructions, as revealed to him by God. We started to pray, and about forty-five minutes into the prayers, I heard my son sneeze. I opened my eyes and then he sneezed again. Then Pastor Matthew said I should go and touch my son's feet with my palms and we continued praying. Then I noticed that my son opened one eye, and then the other eye. I was so happy jumping up, while Pastor Matthew kept thanking God because He answered him. That's how my son came back to me.

TO GOD BE THE GLORY!!!

****

Testimonial-3

Apostle Felicia Johnson, San Diego, CA

I had written in my journal about some things concerning my ministry, finances, my car etc. I phoned Prophet Matthew O'Dunlami and he began to release the word of God concerning *insulating, incubating and consecrating* in the Light of God and Blood of Jesus; and being *insulated, incubated* and *consecrated* with the Holy Ghost Power and Fire of God.

From those few words stemmed a series of things that happened. I performed a marriage ceremony on October 30, 2010, representing covenant. On Tuesday morning around 5:00am I was up to pray and felt led to look out of my sliding glass door. As I looked, I saw a man outside with a flashlight, by my car. I looked further and saw a tow truck behind him. I immediately said, "God I know that this man is not coming to take away the car that you gave me." I then ran out of my apartment jumped into my Jeep and drove off. I did not know where I was going and all the time I am talking to the Lord. There was an Apostle that did not live far from me so I went there and she said, "That is your car and God is going to come through."

Making a long story short, I got ready for work and still talking to the Lord I said, "God I will not run from the enemy, especially for something that belongs to me. I need to know what to do to pay these people." Immediately, the Lord brought my younger brother to mind and to call him, telling him what happened. I did not want to go through the humiliation that I knew would come from him, but I obeyed God. Of course he acted just as I knew he would and then he said, "I will call you back after I speak with my wife."

People of God, I needed almost $900 that day! So when my brother called back, he had the sweetest attitude and was so comforting, that I had to look at the phone! He said, "My wife will send the money, we got your back Sis. Don't worry about it." I don't know what his wife said, but I know she is a woman of God and it changed my brother's attitude and apparently humbled him. Glory to God! The Lord said to me, "I was *insulating, incubating* and *consecrating* you and all that concerns you."

I meditated on that word and by Friday of that same week the Lord sent me to a church that I had never been to before. I thought that I was going to meet a man of God that was allowing me to use his facility for a revival service, yet God had another plan. I arrived, yet didn't see the Bishop and only recognized a few faces. The Minister that was in charge recognized me and introduced me, yet I still didn't know what was going on. The Bishop's wife gets up and says, "The Apostle is in the house and I know she has a word for us. The Bishop just left this morning to go to Missouri and we have been praying that God would send us someone to bless the people in his absence."

I had officially been set up by God. Immediately, He brings forth that word on *insulating, incubating* and *consecrating* using the story of the three Hebrew boys to explain and bless the people of God. I was in awe at how God moved that night and encouraged the people with a word that I had received from Prophet Matthew a week before and God was still performing His Word.

The people were elated and invited me to come and preach on that Sunday because of what they received from God on Friday night. The testimonies of healing and deliverance from the people on the following Sunday was amazing. God had brought change to that body of believers. We were able to go on and have a successful revival the following week and God has been moving ever since.

I thank God for Prophet Matthew and the ministry that God has given to this Man of God. Our meeting from the beginning was God ordained and God has been increasing since that day. We give God the Praise and the Glory for what he will continue to do through this yielded vessel.

****

Testimonial-4

Tracey Williams, Birmingham, MI

It is amazing how God has people cross paths for His purposes. What may seem insignificant turns into a life changing event and then an everlasting friendship. How Matthew and I even crossed paths is a miracle in itself, of which I won't go into detail. Matthew resides in New Jersey and I live in Michigan, with no common friends, relatives or acquaintances. Yet is truly a testimony of when God seeks to pour his favor and Grace upon one of His precious children, all things are possible. God used Matthew, to help deliver me from a bondage that plagued me for years.

After we made our acquaintance, Matthew would often call to pray for or with me. He always had a word to share and his willingness to offer guidance, wisdom and wash me with the word was comforting, as he often proclaimed himself to be my "big brother". Comforting, not only because it was God's word but also as a relatively eager, yet immature Christian, I knew I had a lot to learn. I greatly appreciated the amount of personal time Matthew used to counsel and encourage me. Often, he was willing to spend hours with me, at a local Chinese restaurant, to use the word for the renewing of my mind. Of course this wasn't limited to me, as he often would start a conversation with someone else and then counsel or pray for them, on the spot. Simply, Matthew demonstrated his desire to please God and share God's love with others.

Yet in all this talking, there were some things that I did not share. Not seeking to purposely defraud or omit, yet some things were so much a part of my life, it just didn't occur to me to share what had kept me bound mentally and emotionally for eight years. Since 2001, I had been plagued with a most unusual manifestation of Obsessive Compulsive Disorder - haircutting. Each day, at least several times a day I would retreat to the bathroom and cut my hair to make sure each and every hair was perfectly even. When I wasn't at home to cut my hair, I would obsess about it and constantly "measure" my hair with my fingers to find areas where my hair wasn't perfectly even. Many times, I would spend hours in the bathroom trying to get my hair just 'perfect', only to fall to my knees crying for God to help me stop.

In my own efforts, I would pray or try breaking the habit for twenty one days. Then I would try thirty days. Everyone knows you can break a bad habit by not doing for at least twenty one days, right? Then I sought the help of a therapist, while helpful, still I was bound. As much as I desired to be done with this seemingly insurmountable stronghold, I had also learned to live with it, for eight years.

One day, Matthew calls me out of the blue, as he often does. Yet this time, he pronounced "The day of your deliverance will come! According to Acts chapter ten, like Cornelius, the Lord has heard your prayers and alms. On the ninth day, at the ninth hour, you will receive your deliverance!" Bewildered, I said "Amen" yet not really understanding what he was talking about. So, I forgot about it and went about life. That following month, on the ninth of August at around nine in the morning, I proceeded to the bathroom to get ready for work and perform my morning haircutting ritual. Yet this time, as I entered the bathroom and looked in the mirror, all of a sudden I had a shift in my thinking and just didn't feel like cutting my hair anymore. So, I turned around and left the bathroom. I was done. It was awhile before I even realized it was all according to what Matthew had prayed for me. My day of deliverance really did come, on the ninth day and at the ninth hour! PRAISE THE LORD! HALLELUJAH!

So, more than a year later, my hair continues to grow, long and beautiful. Praise God, for He truly is our healer and deliverer. Also, I praise God for bringing His servant Matthew into my life to pray for me as my big brother, in the spirit. An awesome man of God in whose friendship I treasure.

****

Testimonial-5

Matthew O'Dunlami, Sicklerville, NJ,

I have many testimonies to share even before writing this book, but the most significant one that prompts me to write this prayer book is my experience with the power of God; which gives me ability to see and hear things, manifested by engaging in dynamic prayers. On this particular day, He revealed to me in a dream, from a large crowd, He was set amidst thousands of people, forcefully demanding from Him, without reasoning. He holds nothing in His hand and is the tallest among the crowd, standing about 12ft tall. While everyone was making their vigorous demands from Him, I stood there in the midst of them, all but close enough and I said to Him, ***"I will not take anything from you, unless I fast and pray for it first."*** He was shocked to hear such a profound statement from among this forceful, large crowd.

Suddenly, a white board dropped down from the sky and He wrote my name in the center of this white board. I asked myself, how did this man know my name? At that moment, He turned to me while everyone was totally quiet and He said, ***"Matthew O'Dunlami, from today on, you will never struggle with anyone or with anything in your life again. You have got yours."*** I was shocked to hear His response to me while He quietly laid down. Still He had nothing in His hands to give to anyone except the ***"Word"***, which I had just received from Him. Everyone dispatched from this place and I woke up and thanked Almighty God.

This is the beginning of how my Father taught me how to wait on Him, in prayer and fasting. Jesus said to his disciples, **"'However, this kind does not go out except by prayer and fasting.'"** (Matthew 20:21)

Since then, my prayer life has changed tremendously, and things began to manifest in my life that I couldn't have imagined before. An open heaven occurs on a daily basis, since I started to receive from Him; Scriptures, prayers and even the teaching and instruction of His Word. I thank the Almighty God for this privilege of counting me worthy as a custodian of His Word. Praise the Lord.

****

Holy Spirit Manufactured Prayer

Daily Devotional Prayers
Day 1 through 31

DAY 1

"If My people who are called by My name will humble themselves, and pray and seek My face, and turn from their wicked ways, then I will hear from heaven, and will forgive their sin and heal their land."

2 Chronicles 7:14

"And from the days of John the Baptist until now the kingdom of heaven suffers violence, and the violent take it by force."

Matthew 11:12

Names of Our Lord Jesus Christ:

➤ **Adam:** "And so it is written, the first man Adam was made a living soul; the last Adam was made a quickening spirit." (1 Corinthians 15:45)

➤ **Advocate:** "My little children, these things I write unto you, that ye sin not. And if any man sin, we have an advocate with the Father, Jesus Christ the righteous." (1 John 2:1)

➤ **Almighty:** "I am the Alpha and Omega, the Beginning and the End," says the Lord, "who is and who was and who is to come, the Almighty." (Revelation 1:8)

Declarations and Confessions:

• I receive the key of the house of David, to open the door of anointing.

• I receive the key of the house of David, to open the door of Apostolic gifts.

• I receive the key of the house of David, to open the door of Blessings.

➤ I receive the key of the house of David, to lockup the door of all sin.

➤ I receive the key of the house of David, to lockup the door of bitterness.

➢ I receive the key of the house of David, to lockup the door of bondage.

∞ I am God's child. (John 1:12)

∞ I am Christ's friend. (John 15:15)

❖ **Light of God,** insulate me, incubate me and consecrate me.

❖ **Fire of God,** insulate me, incubate me and consecrate me.

❖ **Blood of Jesus,** insulate me, incubate me and consecrate me.

❖ **Holy Ghost Power,** insulate me, incubate me and consecrate me.

(Scriptures: Gen. 1:3; 1:14, Dan. 3:19-25, 1 Pet. 1:2, Act. 1:8; 2:1-4)

Song of Praises:

Praises, Worship and Thanksgiving (Submit yourself to the Lord)

Example below:

"Amen Amen!! Blessing and Glory,

Wisdom Thanksgiving and Honor,

Power and Might, Be unto our God,

Forever and Ever, Amen.!" (Rev. 7:12)

Prayers:

1. **Yahweh Jireh,** my Provider, according to Your Word let the Abrahamic Covenant reign forever in my life and all that concerns me, in the mighty Name of Jesus. (Gen. 12:1-3; 17:1-10)

2. **El Olam**, Everlasting God, Almighty God of Heaven; all Covenants You established with Abraham, Isaac and Jacob, allow me by Your grace and mercy to be a partaker of these ancient covenants, in Jesus' Name. (Gen. 12:1-3; 17:1-10)

3. **Elohim**, the Strong One, the Almighty God of Heaven; as You changed Jacob's name to Israel, my Father, endow me with Your power and strength to prevail in all things, for Your kingdom, in Jesus' Name. (Gen. 32:24-28)

4. **Yahweh Rapha**, my God who heals, my great physician; come into my life and remove all infirmity, disease, illness, sickness, shame, lack, poverty, and reproach, from me and my life, both spiritually and physically, in the mighty Name of Jesus. (Acts 10:38)

5. **Yahweh Tsidkenu**, the Righteous One; Jesus Christ, cover me and everything connected to me with Your holy garments, of glory and beauty, in the mighty Name of Jesus. (Exod. 28:2)

6. **Adonai**, Lord of All, today wipe out with your precious blood, all strange gods and idols around me. Clean me and change my garments, in the Name of Jesus. (Gen. 35:2)

7. **El Roi**, my God who sees, King of kings, Lord of lords, Ancient of days; anoint me to understand mysteries and secrets behind your words, for the expansion of Your kingdom, in Jesus' Name. (Deut. 4:19)

8. **Yahweh Shalom**, the Lord is my Peace, Almighty God; I receive the royal keys of the Kingdom of Heaven; to bind on earth what is bound in Heaven, and to loose on earth all that is loosed in Heaven, in Jesus' Name. (Matt. 16:19)

9. **Yahweh Shammah**, the GOD who is present; as You did for the three Hebrew children, today my Father insulate, incubate and consecrate me by Your light, fire, blood and Holy Spirit, in the mighty Name of Jesus. (Lev. 8:33-35)

10. Lord Jesus, You separated from Joseph and Mary in Jerusalem to learn, to listen and to question about Your Word. Separate me from those who would not let me learn at Your feet, in the mighty Name of Jesus. (Luke 2:41-50)

11. **Yahweh El Gemolah**, the Lord of recompense; let Your Holy Spirit overshadow me to give birth to good

news and greatness in my life, like you did to Mary, in Jesus' Name. (Luke 1:34; Jer. 51:56)

12. **El Elyon**, the God Most High, Almighty God of Heaven; I ask that You give me Your quick, willing Spirit; like lights, that reveal the mysteries of Heaven to me; to dominate and occupy this earth for the purpose and expansion of Your kingdom, in the mighty Name of Jesus. (Gen. 1:26)

13. **Yahweh Nakeh**, God who smites; today, O whirlwind of God, go forth now, to all four corners of this world; scattering principalities, powers, rulers of the darkness of this age and spiritual hosts of wickedness in heavenly places that are hampering or hindering my destiny and the destiny of my family, in the mighty Name of Jesus. (Eph. 6:12, Jer. 49:36)

14. **Yahweh M'qaddishkhem,** the Lord my Sanctifier, King of kings and Lord of lords; increase my faith, love, and holiness, in the mighty Name of Jesus. (Luke 17:5-6)

15. Holy Ghost and Fire, I denounce and reject completely today, that I will not remain in a temporary place permanently, in the mighty Name of Jesus. (Exod. 12:40-42)

16. Lord Jesus, I decree and receive total balance, in every area of my life, in the mighty Name of Jesus. (Dan. 1:20; 3:22-25)

17. EL Shaddai, the God of my strength and my Father, today I ask You to change my garments from: shame to honor, loss to victory, sickness to health, poverty to wealth, bad to good, lack to abundance, weakness to greatness, failure to success, opposition to victory, scars to stars, bondage to freedom, negative to positive, darkness to light, trials to triumphs, failure to promotion, tests to testimonies, oppression to deliverance, fear to boldness and weakness to strength, in the mighty Name of Jesus. (Exod. 15:27, Rev. 7:16-17)

DAY 2

"He shall call upon Me, and I will answer him; I will be with him in trouble; I will deliver him and honor him. With long life I will satisfy him, And show him My Salvation".

Psalm 91:15

Names of Our Lord Jesus Christ:

➢ **Alpha and Omega:** "I am The Alpha and Omega, the Beginning and the Ending, saith the Lord, which is, and which was, and which is to come, the Almighty." (Revelation 1:8)

➢ **Amen:** "And unto the angel of the church of the Laodiceans write, These things saith The Amen, the faithful and true Witness, the beginning of the creation of God." (Revelation 3:14)

➢ **Apostle of our profession:** "Wherefore, holy brethren, partakers of the heavenly calling, consider the Apostle and High Priest of our profession, Christ Jesus." (Hebrews 3:1)

Declarations and Confessions:

• I receive the key of the house of David, to open the door of deliverance.

• I receive the key of the house of David, to open the door of discernment.

• I receive the key of the house of David, to open the door of pleasing God.

➢ I receive the key of the house of David, to lockup the door of carousing.

> ➤ I receive the key of the house of David, to lockup the door of covetousness.
> ➤ I receive the key of the house of David, to lockup the door of demonic activities.

∞ I am united with the Lord. (1 Corinthians 6:17)

∞ I am bought with a price. (1 Corinthians 6:19-20)

❖ **Light of God,** insulate me, incubate me and consecrate me.

❖ **Fire of God,** insulate me, incubate me and consecrate me.

❖ **Blood of Jesus,** insulate me, incubate me and consecrate me.

❖ **Holy Ghost Power,** insulate me, incubate me and consecrate me.

(Scriptures: Gen. 1:3; 1:14, Dan. 3:19-25, 1 Pet. 1:2, Act. 1:8; 2:1-4)

Song of Praises:

Praises, Worship and Thanksgiving (Submit yourself to the Lord).

Prayers:

1. Zion of Israel, I will not remain in a temporary place permanently. My Father, direct my path today, to the land of permanent dominion, in Jesus' Name. (Gen. 1:26)

2. God, according to the Noahic Covenant which You made with him; my Lord, make me fruitful to multiply and bring forth abundantly on earth, for perpetual generations, in the Name of Jesus. (Gen. 9:12-17)

3. Lord my God, let Your wrath burn hot against my adversaries and the king Herod in my life, and my family's life, in the Name of Jesus. (Exod. 32:11)

4. Lord God in Heaven, purge me and heal me from everything that represents leprosy or uncleanness in my life. Make me whole and clean, to proclaim Your kingdom, in Jesus' Name. (Mark 1:40-42)

5. Lord Jesus Christ, I completely remove all mourning garments from me, my spouse and my children, by the power in the Name of Jesus. (Gen. 38:14-19)

6. Lord, the Alpha and Omega, anoint me with Your great power. Perfect me, establish me, strengthen me, and settle me, for the expansion of Your kingdom, in Jesus' Name. (1 Peter 5:10)

7. Almighty God, today I receive the precious keys of Your kingdom in holiness and righteousness, in the mighty Name of Jesus. (Luke 1:75; Eph. 4:24; Rom. 6:19)

8. Lord Jesus, You separated from Joseph and Mary in Jerusalem, to listen, to learn and ask questions about Your Word. Today, separate me from those who would keep me from learning and discussing Your word, in Jesus' Name. (Luke 2:41-50)

9. Holy Spirit, fill me and rest upon me, like You did to the disciples on the day of Pentecost, in Jesus' Name. (Acts 2:1-6)

10. Almighty God of Heaven, remove from me, the mindset of this earth and replace it totally with the spiritual mindset of Heaven, in the mighty Name of Jesus. (2 Pet. 3:7)

11. Lord God, today I receive the precious spiritual warfare weapon, the Sword of the Spirit; to destroy all wickedness and darkness that comes against me, in Jesus' Name. (Matt. 10:34)

12. My Lord, my Strength, train my hands for war, and my fingers for battle, in the mighty Name of Jesus. (Ps. 144:1)

13. King of kings, Lord of lords, plant seeds of faith in my heart and uproot every obstacle or hindrance to fulfilling my destiny, in Jesus' Name. (Luke 17:5-6).

14. My Lord, let my enemies be ashamed and greatly troubled. Let them turn back from me and suddenly be ashamed, in the Name of Jesus. (Ps. 6:10)

15. God of Israel, Mystery of the Earth; purge out by fire, every one of my blessings residing on the ground, in the mighty Name of Jesus. (Ps. 104:24)

16. Almighty God, Mystery of the Earth; today, swallow-up every trouble and mountain in my life, in the Name of Jesus. (Ps. 104:24)

17. O Lord I decree; violence, wasting and destruction shall cease completely, from my land and my descendant's land, in the Name of Jesus. (Isa. 60: 18)

18. LORD, Mystery of Moon; start working for me today, everywhere I go, in the Name of Jesus. (Isa. 60:19; Ps. 104:24)

19. LORD, today You Mystery of Sun, start working for me. My Father, from today onward, You shall be my everlasting Light, for me and all my descendants, in Jesus' Name. (Isa. 61:19)

20. My God, from generation to generation, Your glory shall be my everlasting Sun, in Jesus' Name. (Isa. 61:20)

DAY 3

"The sacrifice of the wicked is an abomination to the LORD, But the prayer of the upright is His delight."

Proverbs 15:8

Names of Our Lord Jesus Christ:

➢ **Arm of the Lord:** "Awake, awake, put on strength O arm of the LORD! Awake as in the ancient days, in the generations of old. Art thou not it that hath cut Rahab, and wounded the dragon? Who hath believed our report? and to whom is the arm of the LORD revealed?" (Isaiah 51:9, 53:1)

➢ **Author and Finisher of our faith:** "Looking unto Jesus the author and finisher of our faith; who for the joy that was set before Him endured the cross, despising the shame, and is set down at the right hand of the throne of God." (Hebrews 12:2)

➢ **Author of eternal salvation:** "And being made per-fect, He became the author of eternal salvation unto all them that obey Him." (Hebrews 5:9)

Declarations and Confessions:

• I receive the key of the house of David, to open the door of encounters with God.

• I receive the key of the house of David, to open the door of encounters with Jesus.

• I receive the key of the house of David, to open the door of encounters with Holy Spirit.

➢ I receive the key of the house of David, to lockup the door of all diseases.

➢ I receive the key of the house of David, to lockup the door of disobedience.

➢ I receive the key of the house of David, to lockup the door of disregard for others.

∞ I am a saint (set apart for God). (Ephesians 1:1)

∞ I am a personal witness for Christ. (Acts 1:8)

❖ **Light of God,** insulate me, incubate me and consecrate me.

❖ **Fire of God,** insulate me, incubate me and consecrate me.

❖ **Blood of Jesus,** insulate me, incubate me and consecrate me.

❖ **Holy Ghost Power,** insulate me, incubate me and consecrate me.

(Scriptures: Gen. 1:3; 1:14, Dan. 3:19-25, 1 Pet. 1:2, Act. 1:8; 2:1-4))

Song of Praises:

Praises, Worship and Thanksgiving (Submit yourself to the Lord)

Prayers:

1. My Father, as an heir of Abraham, I am a great nation, I am blessed, my name shall be great and be blessed, those who bless me shall be blessed. Those who curse me shall be cursed and through me, all the earth shall be blessed, in the mighty Name of Jesus. (Gen. 12: 1-3)

2. Lord God, as You established Your covenant with Abraham, David and New Covenant; my Lord, establish me, my seed and their seed, for an everlasting covenant, in Jesus' Name. (Gen. 17:7)

3. Lord my God, use Your great power and Your mighty Hand to remove me from the valley of dead bones: poverty, shame, sickness, lack, and unfruitfulness in this world, in Jesus' Name. (Exod. 32:11)

4. Lord Jesus, go forth today and heal each of my destiny helpers, in the four corners of the world. Bring them to help me and equip me with mighty faith, like the centurion man, in Jesus' Name. (Matt. 8:5-13)

5. Father of Light, let me shine in the light of Your countenance, every day of my life, to increase Your kingdom on earth, in Jesus Name. (Luke 24:4)

6. Creator of heaven and earth, let Your Holy Spirit hover over me and bring forth Your light upon me, in order

to understand those things that are hidden, in Jesus' Name. (Gen.1:3-5;14-16)

7. Jehovah God, I use the key of the house of David to open doors of encounter with You, with the Lord Jesus and with the Holy Spirit; that I will be encouraged to endure and bring many souls to salvation, for Your kingdom, in Jesus' Name. (Isa. 22:22)

8. Father, separate me from those who would not let me grow in wisdom and knowledge of You and send them on a long journey away from me, in the mighty Name of Jesus. (Luke 2: 41-44)

9. Jesus Christ my Savior, I decree by the power in Your Name, the desire to mind Your business first will always be in my heart, each day of my life, in the mighty Name of Jesus. (Luke 2:49)

10. Holy Spirit, use my tongue to give utterances like on the day of Pentecost, in the Name of Jesus. (Acts 2:2-3)

11. Lord God, open my eyes to see mysteries in Your word, to expand the Kingdom of God on earth, in the mighty Name of Jesus. (Luke 24-13-34)

12. Mighty God of Heaven, I receive Your royal stone from Heaven to cast down by fire, the prince of the kingdom of Persia flying over my destiny, in the mighty Name of Jesus. (Isa. 14:29)

13. My Lord Jesus Christ, You know the hearts of all things; show me clearly through Your Holy Spirit every decision I am to make in my life and in my ministry, in Jesus' Name. (Acts 1:24-25)

14. Almighty God of Israel, today, I decree from the four corners of the world, as Wise men located Jesus Christ's Star and followed Him to bless Him in His location; those who would bless me will locate my stars and come to my location in order to bless me, in the mighty Name of Jesus. (Matt. 2:1-12)

15. Almighty, Mystery of Earth, today swallow up every trouble and mountain in my life, in the mighty Name of Jesus. (2 Sam. 22:7-8)

16. Mighty God, Mystery of Water, rain abundant blessings on my ground and bring forth the goodness and fruitfulness of the land to me, in the mighty Name of Jesus. (Deut. 22:1-3)

17. Mighty God of Heaven, in my life and descendant to come, I will be served first in every area of my life and I denounce and cancel any leftovers completely, in the mighty Name of Jesus. (Matt 15:22-28, Dan.1:4-21)

18. Yahweh Raah, the Lord my Shepherd; as you accepted Abel's offering, endow me with the key to your Respect Offering, that will bring Your glory down in my life and descendant lives, in Jesus' Name. (Gen. 4:3)

DAY 4

"And when you pray, you shall not be like hypocrites. For they love to pray standing in the synagogues and on the corners of the streets, that they may be seen by men. Assuredly, I say to you, they have their reward."

"But you, when you pray, go into your room, and when you have shut your door, pray to your Father who is in the secret place; and your Father who sees in secret will reward you openly."

Matthew 6:5-6

Names of Our Lord Jesus Christ:

➢ **Beginning of Creation God:** "And unto the angel of the church of the Laodiceans write, these things saith the Amen, the faithful and true witness, the beginning of the creation of God." (Revelation 3:14)

➢ **Beloved Son:** "Behold my servant, whom I have chosen, my beloved, in whom my soul is well pleased. I will put My Spirit upon Him, and He shall show judgment to the Gentiles." (Matthew 12:18)

➢ **Blessed and Only Potentate:** "Which in his times he shall show, who is the blessed and only Potentate, the King of kings, and Lord of lords." (1 Timothy 6:15)

Declarations and Confessions:

• I receive the key of the house of David, to open the door of encouragement.

• I receive the key of the house of David, to open the door of endurance.

• I receive the key of the house of David, to open the door of evangelism.

➢ I receive the key of the house of David, to lockup the door of dissensions.

➢ I receive the key of the house of David, to lockup the door of drunkenness.

➤ I receive the key of the house of David, to lockup the door of envy.

∞ I am free forever from condemnation. (Romans 8: 1-2)

∞ I am a citizen of Heaven. I am significant. (Philippians 3:20)

❖ **Light of God,** insulate me, incubate me and consecrate me.

❖ **Fire of God,** insulate me, incubate me and consecrate me.

❖ **Blood of Jesus,** insulate me, incubate me and consecrate me.

❖ **Holy Ghost Power,** insulate me, incubate me and consecrate me.

(Scriptures: Gen. 1:3; 1:14, Dan. 3:19-25, 1 Pet. 1:2, Act. 1:8; 2:1-4)

Song of Praises:

Praises, Worship and Thanksgiving (Submit yourself to the Lord)

Prayers:

1. Almighty God, forgive all my sins known and unknown, from my mother's stomach, in the mighty Name of Jesus. (1 John 1:7)

2. Almighty God, direct my path and my destiny to walk before You and be blameless, in Jesus' Name. (Gen.17:1-2)

3. God of Israel, as You said to Abraham, David and the New Covenant; let Your covenant remain with me and establish me and my seed, in all their descendant for-ever, in Jesus' Name. (Gen. 17:9-19)

4. Jehovah God, as You put Your word in Balaam's mouth, today my God, let Your word remain in my mouth all the days of my life; and will not curse those whom You have blessed, in Jesus' Name. (Num. 22: 38)

5. Lord Jesus, today come in to my spiritual and physical house and heal all weaknesses in my body and my finances; just like You did for Peter's mother- in-law, in Jesus' Name. (Matt. 8:14-15, John 4:18-19)

6. Lord Jesus, let my garments always be white and never let my head lack the oil of anointing, in the Name of Jesus. (Eccles. 9:8)

7. Almighty God, give me Your quick willing spirit that transmits mysteries from heaven to me on earth; to dominate for the purpose and expansion of Your Kingdom, in Jesus' Name. (Gen. 1:26)

8. Almighty God, I use the key of David to open the doors of: faith, faithfulness, favor, gentleness, giving, glory, crucifixion of the flesh, goodness, mercies, greatness, and healings, in Jesus' Name. (Isa. 22:22; Matt. 16:19)

9. Jesus Christ my Savior, I decree by the power of Your Name, the desire to mind Your business first will be in my heart, every day of my life, in the mighty Name of Jesus. (Luke 2:49)

10. Lord Jesus, I claim increase in Your Word and Understanding. My Father, let me grow in Wisdom, Stature and in Favor with God and men, in the mighty Name of Jesus. (Luke: 2:52)

11. Holy Spirit uproot by fire and bury permanently, every evil tree planted in my life, in Jesus' Name. (Mark 11:12-14, 20-22, John 1:45-51)

12. Lord of Heaven, open my eyes O Lord, to see myself as You see me in Your Kingdom, in the mighty Name of Jesus. (Job 29:15, Ps 34:15, Isa, 6:5, Luke 24:31)

13. Lord Jesus, I arrest every spiritual attacker and manipulation coming to me through dreams. I pray they all

dissolve and I paralyze their activities today, in the Name of Jesus. (Zech. 14:12)

14. My Lord Jesus, Son of David, remove by fire every hindrance in my relationship with You. Open my eyes to see You and the hidden manna, in Jesus' Name. (Mark 10:47, Rev 2:17)

15. O' Lord, open my eyes to see myself as you see me from Your throne, in Jesus Name. (Job 29:15, Ps 34:15, Isa, 6:5, Luke 24:31)

16. O' Lord, open my eyes to see you God, everyday and in every area of my life, in Jesus' Name. (Job 29:15, Ps 34:15, Isa, 6:5, Luke 24:31)

17. O' Lord open my eyes to see the enemies of my life and where they are hidden, in Jesus' Name. (2 Kings 6:17)

18. O' Lord, open my eyes to see the enemies of my life and give me strategies to use against them, in Jesus' Name. (2 Kings 6:17)

19. O' Lord, open my eyes to see where I am today, in the mighty Name of Jesus. (1 Peter 3:13)

20. O' Lord open my eyes to see where I am going on my destiny road, in Jesus' Name. (Num. 22:31)

DAY 5

"However, this kind does not go out except by prayer and fasting."

Matthew 17:21

Names of Our Lord Jesus Christ:

➤ **Branch:** "In that day shall the branch of the LORD be beautiful and glorious, and the fruit of the earth shall be excellent and comely for them that are escaped of Israel." (Isaiah 4:2)

➤ **Bread of Life:** "Then Jesus said unto them, verily, verily, I say unto you, Moses gave you not that bread from heaven; but my Father giveth you the true bread from heaven." (John 6:32)

➤ **Captain of Salvation:** "For it became him, for whom are all things, and by whom are all things, in bringing many sons unto glory, to make the captain of their salvation perfect through sufferings." (Hebrews 2:10)

Declarations and Confessions:

• I receive the key of the house of David, to open the door of faith.

• I receive the key of the house of David, to open the door of faithfulness.

• I receive the key of the house of David, to open the door of favor.

➤ I receive the key of the house of David, to lockup the door of evil spirits.

➢ I receive the key of the house of David, to lockup the door of excessiveness.

➢ I receive the key of the house of David, to lockup the door of factions.

∞ I am free from any charge against me. (Romans 8:31-34)

∞ I am a minister of reconciliation for God. (2 Corinthians 5:17-21)

❖ **Light of God,** insulate me, incubate me and conse-crate me.

❖ **Fire of God,** insulate me, incubate me and consecrate me.

❖ **Blood of Jesus,** insulate me, incubate me and conse-crate me.

❖ **Holy Ghost Power,** insulate me, incubate me and con-secrate me.

(Scriptures: Gen. 1:3; 1:14, Dan. 3:19-25, 1 Pet. 1:2, Act. 1:8; 2:1-4)

Song of Praises:

Praises, Worship and Thanksgiving (Submit yourself to the Lord)

Prayers:

1. Almighty God, remember Your Covenants with Abraham, Isaac, Jacob and me. Today I ask, let these Covenants multiply me exceedingly to increase your Kingdom, in Jesus' Name. (Gen 17:1-8, Deut. 1:11)

2. Lord Jesus Christ, by the Covenant in the parables of: mustard seeds, leavened bread, yeast, hidden treasures, pearls of a great price and a net cast into the sea; begin to work and expand the kingdom of God in my life, in Jesus' Name. (Mark 4:30-33, Matt. 13:44-52)

3. Jehovah God, open my eyes of understanding so that I will see and hear the power of Your glory. Father, no animal will speak to me before I hear and see you, in the Name of Jesus. (Num. 22:28-33)

4. My Lord Jesus, hear my cry from afar and locate me in the place of my trouble; heal all my infirmities since I was born and replace them totally with the Kingdom of God, in Jesus' Name. (Mark 5:1-15)

5. Lord Jesus, every enemy of my household that has stolen my garments and divided into four parts; let all my garments and all that concerns me receive the Blood of Jesus, in the Name of Jesus. (John 19:23)

6. Almighty God, in your Mercy and Grace is your Word. Let Your Light shine all Your spoken parables unto my heart and grant me understanding, for the expansion of your Kingdom, in Jesus' Name. (Rev. 7:12)

7. Lord Jesus, every Word that I: sow, see, read, hear and minister will not be found on the wayside, in stony places, or in thorny places; but will reside in good soil and germinate, in Jesus' Name. (Matt. 13:1-17)

8. The Almighty God, I use the key of the house of David, to open doors to hear: God's voice, holiness, joy, kindness, knowledge, light, longsuffering, love, obedience and opportunity, in Jesus' Name. (Gal. 5:22-23)

9. Lord Jesus, I claim increase in Your Word and Understanding. My Father, let me grow in wisdom, stature and in favor; with God and men, in the mighty Name of Jesus. (Luke 2:52)

10. Holy Ghost, purge out by fire: every disease, illness, lack, shame, poverty, sorrow, tragedy and demonic power, planted in my life and my family's life, in Jesus' Name. (Mark 5:1-20)

11. Lord of Heaven, open my eyes O' Lord, to see God in every area of my life, in the mighty Name of Jesus. (Luke 24:13-34)

12. Jehovah GOD, I retrieve my stolen treasures, virtues, goodness and blessings. Father, let every war of evil

against my destiny, collapse and give up totally, in the Name of Jesus. (1 Kings 5:2-4)

13. LORD God, who made heaven, earth, sea and all that is in them; look at my threats and grant me the boldness to speak your word, like liquid fire, in Jesus' Name. (Acts 4:24-30)

14. The Almighty God, consume by fire today, all impurities in my hands and make me holy in Your presence, all the days of my life and descendant's lives, in the mighty Name of Jesus. (Gen. 3:1-13; Gen. 35: 1-7)

15. Jesus Christ, the cup of blessing which You have blessed shall continually commune with me in the Blood of Christ. The bread which You have broken shall continually commune with me in the Body of Christ and remain permanently in my household forever, in Jesus' Name. (1 Corinth. 10:16)

16. Lord Jesus Christ, today, by the power in Your Blood; I denounce and cancel completely, the cup of demons in my life, in the mighty Name of Jesus. (1 Corinth. 10:20-21)

17. Lord, with Your Majestic power, take away by Your hand, the cup of fury and trembling, from my life today. My Father, I receive the cup of Salvation, in the mighty Name of Jesus. (Isa. 51:17, 22; Isa. 12:3)

DAY 6

"O My Father, if it is possible, let this cup pass from Me; nevertheless, not as I will, but as You will."

Matthew 26:39

Names of Our Lord Jesus Christ:

➢ **Chief Shepherd:** "And when the chief Shepherd shall appear, ye shall receive a crown of glory that fadeth not away." (1 Peter 5:4)

➢ **Christ of God:** "He said unto them, But whom say ye that I am? Peter answering said, The Christ of God." (Luke 9:20)

➢ **Consolation of Israel:** "And, behold, there was a man in Jerusalem, whose name was Simeon; and the same man was just and devout, waiting for the consolation of Israel: and the Holy Ghost was upon him." (Luke 2:25)

Declarations and Confessions:

• I receive the key of the house of David, to open the door of gentleness.

• I receive the key of the house of David, to open the door of giving.

• I receive the key of the house of David, to open the door of glory.

➢ I receive the key of the house of David, to lockup the door of Galatians 5:19-21.

➢ I receive the key of the house of David, to lockup the door of gluttony.

➢ I receive the key of the house of David, to lockup the door of gossip.

∞ I have access to God through the Holy Spirit. (Ephesians 2:18)

∞ I am seated with Christ in the heavenly realms. (Ephesians 2:6)

❖ **Light of God,** insulate me, incubate me and consecrate me.

❖ **Fire of God,** insulate me, incubate me and consecrate me.

❖ **Blood of Jesus,** insulate me, incubate me and consecrate me.

❖ **Holy Ghost Power,** insulate me, incubate me and consecrate me.

(Scriptures: Gen. 1:3; 1:14, Dan. 3:19-25, 1 Pet. 1:2, Act. 1:8; 2:1-4)

Song of Praises:

Praises, Worship and Thanksgiving (Submit yourself to the Lord)

Prayers:

1. My Father, the Mighty One of Israel: as You changed Abram's name to Abraham, Jacob's name to Israel, Simon's name to Peter, and Saul's name to Paul; change my name to establish and re-align me with Your covenant forever, in Jesus' Name. (Gen. 17:1-8)

2. My God, I denounce all wrong covenants with false gods and idols of any kind, created by my ancestors. Today, I claim the precious blood covenant of Jesus Christ, in my life, in the mighty Name of Jesus. (Exod. 23:32; 34:15)

3. King of kings, Lord of lords, in wisdom and power, You created this world. Today, endow me with Your abundant wisdom, knowledge and revelation power; to walk and work in Your Kingdom effectively, in Jesus' Name. (Eph. 3:10; Rom. 11:33; 2 Chron.1:10)

4. My Lord Jesus, today I destroy and break every evil yoke and demonic covenant trying to dominate my life and my family. I align myself with the Kingdom of God, in Jesus' Name. (Mark 5:1-15, Matt. 17:14-18)

5. Lord Jesus Christ, the Son of the Living God, I reject and refuse to have my riches be corrupted. My garments and my linens will not be moth-eaten, in the mighty Name of Jesus. (James 5:2)

6. Lord Jesus, I pray that every word, offering and service that I sow, see, read, hear and minister will not be found on the way side, in stony places, or in thorny places; but will be found in good soil and germinating, in Jesus' Name. (Matt. 13:1-17)

7. The Almighty God, I use the key of the house of David to open doors, as an Oracle of God: pastoral gifts, patience, peace, power, prophetic gifts, prosperity, scriptures, visions and seeing God, in Jesus' Name. (Isa. 22:22)

8. Mighty God of Heaven, breathe through me the same Spirit of wisdom and understanding You breathed into the ancient men, who were inspired to write Your scripture, in the mighty Name of Jesus. (Isa. 11:2-3)

9. Lord that answers by fire; today, consume the works of darkness planned against me to impede my destiny and journey to greatness, in Jesus' Name. (1 Kings 18:38, 2 kings 1:12)

10. Lord of Heaven, open my eyes O Lord, to see the people surrounding me, in every area of my life, in the mighty Name of Jesus. (Luke 24:13-34)

11. My Heavenly Father, let all spiritual animals: cats, dogs, goats, spiders, snakes, crocodiles and dragons paraded against me, be chained and returned to the senders by Fire and by the Blood of Jesus. Let all

arrows, gunshots, wounds, harassments, initiations, intimidations, attacks, and oppositions; both physically and spiritually, be returned to the sender, in the Name of Jesus. (2 Kings 9:30-37; Rev. 2:20-23)

12. Lord God who made Heaven, earth and sea; support me by stretching out Your hand, to heal me during persecutions. Let signs and wonders follow me, in Jesus name. (Acts 4:24-30)

13. Lord Jesus, I will eat with kings and presidents, of all nations on this earth, in the mighty Name of Jesus. (1 Peter 2:9; Esther 5:1-6)

14. My Lord, in this Christian race, I will finish and I will end well. I have victory over satan. satan will not truncate my destiny, in the mighty Name of Jesus. (Esther 5:1-8)

15. Mighty God of Heaven, by the power in your Blood, I denounce and cancel, every disease and plague of the land; from touching me, my family or my descendants, in Jesus' Name. (Exod. 11:1, 12:13)

16. Lord Jesus Christ, keep me from anything polluted by: idols, sexual immorality, things strangled and from blood, in the Name of Jesus. (Deut. 23:22; Acts 15:19-20)

17. Lord Jesus Christ, keep me from every evil and fleshly lust against my soul, in the mighty Name of Jesus. (1 Thess. 5:22; 1 Pet. 2:11)

DAY 7

"Watch and pray, lest you enter into temptation. The Spirit indeed is willing, but the flesh is weak."

Matthew 26:41

Names of Our Lord Jesus Christ:

➢ **Cornerstone:** "The stone which the builders refused is become the head stone of the corner." (Psalms 118:22)

➢ **Counselor:** "For unto us a child is born, unto us a son is given: and the government shall be upon his shoulder: and his name shall be called Wonderful, Counselor, The mighty God, The everlasting Father; the Prince of Peace." (Isaiah 9:6)

➢ **Creator:** "All things were made by him; and without him was not anything made that was made." (John 1:3)

Declarations and Confessions:

• I receive the key of the house of David, to open the door to crucify my flesh.

• I receive the key of the house of David, to open the door of goodness.

• I receive the key of the house of David, to open the door of greatness.

➢ I receive the key of the house of David, to lockup the door of greed.

➢ I receive the key of the house of David, to lockup the door of hostility.

➢ I receive the key of the house of David, to lockup the door of hypocrisy.

∞ I cannot be separated from the love of God. (Romans 8:35-39)

∞ I am established, anointed, sealed by God. (2 Corinthians 1:21-22)

❖ **Light of God,** insulate me, incubate me and consecrate me.

❖ **Fire of God,** insulate me, incubate me and consecrate me.

❖ **Blood of Jesus,** insulate me, incubate me and consecrate me.

❖ **Holy Ghost Power,** insulate me, incubate me and consecrate me.

(Scriptures: Gen. 1:3; 1:14, Dan. 3:19-25, 1 Pet. 1:2, Act. 1:8; 2:1-4)

Song of Praises:

Praises, Worship and Thanksgiving (Submit yourself to the Lord)

Prayers:

1. Almighty God, every good thing my Lot has taken away from me, today I command Your heavenly raven to go forth and bring the goodness of the land to me as you have done to Elijah, in Jesus' Name. (1 Kings 17:1-end)

2. My LORD, remove totally from my household and all that concerns me, the spirit of disobedience, in the Name of Jesus. (Luke 17:32)

3. LORD, God of Israel, endow me with Your power to get wealth, that will establish Your covenant You have spoken concerning Father Abraham, Isaac, Jacob and me, in Jesus' Name. (Deut. 8:18)

4. Lord Jesus, you heard the cry of the man of Gadara, near the tombs. Today come quickly, with Your precious Blood and draw the line to separate me totally, from any power of darkness, in Jesus' Name. (Mark 5:1-15)

5. Almighty God, look unto me and my garments will not be defiled. They shall remain perfect and I will walk in white, every single day of my life, in Jesus' Name. (Rev. 3:4)

6. Lord Jesus, everything I sow will not be found on the wayside to be devoured by birds; nor on stony places

to be dried up; and not on thorny places to be choked; but will be found on good ground, to bring the goodness and fruitfulness of the land to me, in Jesus' Name. (Matt. 13:1-9)

7. Almighty God, I use the key of the house of David to open doors of self control, as a servant of God, for service to God. I will have the mind of God while teaching His word and have the understanding to walk with God, in Jesus' Name. (Eph. 5:1)

8. Almighty God of Heaven, as I compose this word, my heart shall be overflowing with a good theme and my tongue shall be like the pen of a ready writer, in Jesus' Name. (Ps. 45:1)

9. Mighty God of Heaven, I decree everything representing the tares, weeds and evil fig trees in my life and in my family's life; let them wither now, from the root, in Jesus' Name. (Matt. 13:24-30, John 1:48, Mark 11:12-14)

10. Lord of Heaven, open my eyes O' Lord to see where I am today, in every area of my life, in the mighty Name of Jesus. (Luke 24:13-34)

11. Lamb of God, I reject every spiritual load of darkness placed on me. Today I decree, purge my intestines and my blood from satanic foods and injections, in the mighty Name of Jesus. (Dan. 1:12-20)

12. Lord Jesus, remove from me today, a faithless and perverse heart. Equip me with Your Holiness, Holy Ghost Power and Fire, in Jesus' Name. (Matt. 17:15-2)

13. Mighty God from Heaven, I shatter by fire every eye or satanic mirror monitoring my destiny, since the day I was born, in the Name of Jesus. (Zech. 14:12)

14. Holy Ghost and Fire, I take back by fire, every one of the blessings and good things in my life that the enemy of my ancestors has been sitting on, in Jesus' Name. (Gen. 14:1-31, Exod. 15:27)

15. Lion of Judah, today I send you forth to devour, every evil animal holding me back from reaching my destiny, in the mighty Name of Jesus. (2 Kings 9:36-37)

16. My Lord Jesus, I separate by Your Blood, every satanic, genetic re-engineering, in my blood line and replace them completely with the redemptive Blood of Jesus, in the mighty Name of Jesus.

17. My God in battle, I decree, every one of my blessings, in my enemy's hands and houses; today, I purge out by fire and redirect them to my house, in the mighty Name of Jesus. (Gen. 15:27)

18. LORD, all Scriptures are given by Your inspiration. Count them worthy in my life to be profitable for: doctrine, reproof, correction and instruction in righteousness, in Jesus' Name. (2 Tim. 3:16)

DAY 8

"So He said to them when you pray, say: "Our Father in heaven, Hallowed be Your name. Your kingdom come on earth as it is in heaven, Give us day by day our daily bread. And forgive us our sins, For we also forgive everyone who is indebted to us. And do not lead us into temptation, but deliver us from the evil one."

Luke 11:1

Names of Our Lord Jesus Christ:

> **Dayspring:** Through the tender mercy of our God; whereby the dayspring from on high hath visited us. (Luke 1:78)

> **Deliverer:** And so all Israel shall be saved: as it is written, There shall come out of Zion the Deliverer, and shall turn away ungodliness from Jacob. (Romans 11:26)

> **Desire of the nations:** And I will shake all nations, and the desire of all nations shall come: and I will fill this house with glory, saith the LORD of hosts. (Haggai 2:7)

Declarations and Confessions:

- I receive the key of the house of David, to open the door of supernatural healing.
- I receive the key of the house of David, to open the door of hearing from God.
- I receive the key of the house of David, to open the door of Holiness.

> I receive the key of the house of David, to lockup the door of idolatry.

> I receive the key of the house of David, to lockup the door of immorality.

➢ I receive the key of the house of David, to lockup the door of impatience.

∞ I am assured all things work together for good. (Romans 8: 28)

∞ I have been chosen and appointed to bear fruit. (John 15:16)

❖ **Light of God,** insulate me, incubate me and consecrate me.

❖ **Fire of God,** insulate me, incubate me and consecrate me.

❖ **Blood of Jesus,** insulate me, incubate me and consecrate me.

❖ **Holy Ghost Power,** insulate me, incubate me and consecrate me.

(Scriptures: Gen. 1:3; 1:14, Dan. 3:19-25, 1 Pet. 1:2, Act. 1:8; 2:1-4)

Song of Praises:

Praises, Worship and Thanksgiving (Submit yourself to the Lord)

Prayers:

1. Almighty God, today, establish Your Covenant with me to be exceedingly fruitful. Nations and kings will come from me. A stranger's land that I dwell in, will become my land, for everlasting possession, in the Name of Jesus. (Gen. 17:1-8)

2. Lord, remember me and the New Covenant of my ancestors. Every offering shall be seasoned with salt and I will not lack the Salt Covenant of God, in the Name of Jesus. (Lev. 2:13; 26:45)

3. My Lord God, the Great one of Israel, my strength and power; perfect me, establish me, strengthen me and settle me, in all areas of my life, in the mighty Name of Jesus. (2 Sam. 22:33)

4. Prince of Peace, separate me from all sickness, introduced to me by the power of darkness, of this evil world, in Jesus' Name. (Mark 5:1-15)

5. Jesus the King of kings, today I pray every enemy of my destiny that is running after my garments, let them receive blindness and catch fire, in the Name of Jesus. (Matt. 27:35; Mark 15:24)

6. Lord Jesus, the kingdom of God is like a man who sowed good seed in his field, but tares appeared. Holy Ghost and Fire, every tare among my good seeds,

uproot now and be cast into the lake of fire, in Jesus' Name. (Matt. 13:24-30)

7. Almighty God, I use the key of David to open the doors of: wealth, wisdom, vision, knowledge, worship, the praise of God, the Word of God and revelation gifts, in Jesus' Name. (Matt. 16:19)

8. LORD, as You did to Daniel and the Hebrew children, take away from me all delicacies and food from idols. Replace them with Your knowledge, skill, wisdom and the understanding of visions and dreams, in the mighty Name of Jesus. (Dan 1:17)

9. The Ancient of Days, like Peter gave birth to the greatness inside him that let the lame walk; my Lord, let me give birth to the greatness inside me, that will make the lame walk, the blind to see, the deaf to hear and the dumb to talk, in the mighty Name of Jesus. (Acts 3:1-10)

10. LORD of heaven, open my eyes O Lord, to see where I am going in every area of my life, in the mighty Name of Jesus. (Luke 24:13-34)

11. God of Heaven, I break every evil covenant and initiation. I disband all hosts of darkness that are set against me physically and spiritually, in Jesus' Name. (Judg. 15, 16:23-31)

12. Lord Jesus, remove from me today a faithless and perverse heart and replace it with: the power of prayer and fasting; to have all prayers answered; and heal every demonic illness and disease, in Jesus' Name. (Matt.17:15-21)

13. Mighty God, wake up in me, everything that has been dead in my life, by Your resurrection power, in the mighty Name of Jesus. (John 11:25; Phil. 3:10)

14. My Father, wake up in me, everything that has been dead in my Christian journey, with Your resurrection power, in the mighty Name of Jesus. (John11:25; Phil 3:10)

15. My Father, revive my: faith, finances, health, career and spiritual life that has been dead, with Your resurrection power, in the mighty Name of Jesus. (John 11:25; Phil 3:10)

16. LORD God, according to the mystery of the five loaves of bread and two fish; I receive sudden supernatural provision in all areas of my life, to feed nations, in the mighty Name of Jesus. (Mark 6:34-44)

17. LORD God, according to the mystery of the five loaves of bread and two fish; I receive sudden supernatural multiplication and I am complete in every area of my life, in the mighty Name of Jesus. (Mark 6:34-44)

18. LORD God, according to the mystery of the five loaves of bread and two fish; let sudden supernatural increase for all good things, come into my life. I am perfected in every area of my life, in the mighty Name of Jesus. (Mark 6:34-44)

DAY 9

"He spoke a parable to them that men always ought to pray and not to lose heart."

Luke 18:1

Names of Our Lord Jesus Christ:

➤ **Door:** Then said Jesus unto them again, verily, verily, I say unto you, I am the door of the sheep. (John 10:7)

➤ **Elect of God:** Behold my servant, whom I uphold; mine elect, in whom my soul delighteth; I have put my spirit upon him: he shall bring forth judgment to the Gentiles. (Isaiah 42:1)

➤ **Everlasting Father:** For unto us a child is born, unto us a son is given: and the government shall be upon his shoulder: and his name shall be called Wonderful, Counselor, The mighty God, The everlasting Father, The Prince of Peace. (Isaiah 9:6)

Declarations and Confessions:

• I receive the key of the house of David, to open the door of unspeakable joy.

• I receive the key of the house of David, to open the door of kindness.

• I receive the key of the house of David, to open the door of inspiration in God.

➤ I receive the key of the house of David, to lockup the door of improvidence.

➤ I receive the key of the house of David, to lockup the door of impurity.

➢ I receive the key of the house of David, to lockup the door of infirmities.

∞ I may approach God with freedom and confidence. (Ephesians. 3: 12)

∞ I can do all things through Christ who strengthens me. (Philippians 4:13)

❖ **Light of God,** insulate me, incubate me and consecrate me.

❖ **Fire of God,** insulate me, incubate me and consecrate me.

❖ **Blood of Jesus,** insulate me, incubate me and consecrate me.

❖ **Holy Ghost Power,** insulate me, incubate me and consecrate me.

(Scriptures: Gen. 1:3; 1:14, Dan. 3:19-25, 1 Pet. 1:2, Act. 1:8; 2:1-4)

Song of Praises:

Praises, Worship and Thanksgiving (Submit yourself to the Lord)

Prayers:

1. Almighty God, according to your Word, in Isaiah 58, grant me Your four blessings; and today, I receive all 58 blessings in the bible, forever, in the Name of Jesus. (Deut. 28:1-14)

2. Lord God, I will keep the Covenant of God forever and I will walk uprightly, in the Name of Jesus. (Jer. 31:31; Matt 25:28)

3. Almighty God, keep me strong for all battles. Lord, use Your great power to help cast down the enemy before me, by fire, in the Name of Jesus. (2 Chron. 20:6)

4. Lord Jesus, send all my destiny helpers to me from the four corners of the world and take me to your sanctuary of healing; spiritually, physically and financially, in Jesus' Name. (Matt. 9:2-7, Mark 5:18-25)

5. My Lord Jesus, take away all filthy garments from me. Remove my iniquity from me and clothe me with Your rich robes; like you did to Joshua, in Jesus' Name. (Zech. 3:1-5)

6. Almighty God in Heaven, I decree every tree that my Father did not plant in my life, my family's life or in my ministry; be uprooted by fire now, in Jesus' Name. (Matt. 13:24-30)

7. Almighty God, I use the key of the house of David, to lockup: sins, bitterness, bondage, carousing, covetousness, demons, depravity, disease, disobedience and disregard for others, in the Name of Jesus. (Gal. 5:19-21; Rev 2:20-22)

8. My Father in Heaven, bless me O Lord and reveal to me things of heaven which flesh and blood on earth will not reveal to me, in the mighty Name of Jesus. (Matt. 16:17)

9. Holy Ghost, incubate and consecrate me with Your power, like Peter. Ignite me with the fire of the Holy Ghost for when the enemy of the Church comes, to lie and deceive me, in the mighty Name of Jesus. (Acts 5:1-11)

10. My Everlasting Father, according to Your Word, let the seven Spirits of the Lord overshadow me every day of my life, to promote and proclaim the Kingdom of God forever, in Jesus' Name. (Isa. 11:2-3)

11. Mighty God, every evil imagination, doorway and ladder to satanic invasion in my life; now be abolished and catch fire forever, in the mighty Name of Jesus. (Jer. 5:26-27)

12. Jesus of Nazareth during the storms of life, give me a heart of praise, worship, and thanksgiving to your

Holy Name; in all areas of my life, in Jesus' Name. (Matt. 11:25, Luke 10:21)

13. Lord Jesus, according to the mystery of the five loaves of bread and two fish, let Your covenant remain in my life. I proclaim am fruitful in every area of my life, in the mighty Name of Jesus. (Mark 6:34-44)

14. Lord Jesus, according to the mystery of the five loaves of bread and two fish, I receive divine attention, in all areas of my life, in Jesus' Name. (Matt. 13:3-50, Mark 6:34-44)

15. Lord Jesus, according to the mystery of the five loaves of bread and two fish, I receive divine approval, in all areas of my life, in Jesus' Name. (Mark 6:34-44)

16. Lord Jesus, according to the mystery of the five loaves of bread and two fish, I receive divine favor, in all areas of my life, in Jesus' Name. (Mark 6:34-44)

17. Lord Jesus, according to the mystery of the five loaves of bread and two fish, I receive abundant blessings, in all areas of my life, in Jesus' Name. (Mark 6:34-44)

18. Lord Jesus, according to the mystery of the five loaves of bread and two fish, I receive divine attraction and attention, in all areas of my life, in Jesus' Name. (Mark 6:34-44)

19. Lord Jesus, according to the mystery of the five loaves of bread and two fish, I receive a divine partner with

the Lord Jesus Christ's heavenly Kingdom, in all areas of my life, in Jesus' Name. (Mark 6:34-44)

20. Lord Jesus, according to the mystery of the five loaves of bread and two fish, I receive divine reconciliations and consolations, in all areas of my life, in Jesus' Name. (Mark 6:34-44)

DAY 10

"Jesus said; "I pray for them. I do not pray for the world but for those whom You have given Me, for they are Yours. And all Mine are Yours, and Yours are Mine, and I am glorified in them."

John 17:9-10

Names of Our Lord Jesus Christ:

➤ **Faithful Witness:** And from Jesus Christ, who is the faithful witness, and the first begotten of the dead, and the prince of the kings of the earth. Unto him that loved us, and washed us from our sins in his own blood. (Revelation 1:5)

➤ **First and Last:** And when I saw him, I fell at his feet as dead. And he laid his right hand upon me, saying unto me, Fear not; I am the first and the last. (Revelation 1:17)

➤ **First Begotten:** And from Jesus Christ, who is the faithful witness, and the first begotten of the dead, and the prince of the kings of the earth. Unto him that loved us, and washed us from our sins in his own blood. (Revelation 1:5)

Declarations and Confessions:

• I receive the key of the house of David, to open the door of knowledge.
• I receive the key of the house of David, to open the door to the light of God.
• I receive the key of the house of David, to open the door of longsuffering.

> I receive the key of the house of David, to lockup the door of jealousy.
> I receive the key of the house of David, to lockup the door of apathy for the future.
> I receive the key of the house of David, to lockup the door of lack.

∞ I am the branch of the true vine, a channel of His life. (John 15: 1-5)

∞ I am God's temple. (1 Corinthians 3: 16).

❖ **Light of God,** insulate me, incubate me and consecrate me.

❖ **Fire of God,** insulate me, incubate me and consecrate me.

❖ **Blood of Jesus,** insulate me, incubate me and consecrate me.

❖ **Holy Ghost Power,** insulate me, incubate me and consecrate me.

(Scriptures: Gen. 1:3; 1:14, Dan. 3:19-25, 1 Pet. 1:2, Act. 1:8; 2:1-4)

Song of Praises:

Praises, Worship and Thanksgiving (Submit yourself to the Lord)

Prayers:

1. LORD, according to Your Word, every one of my blessings stolen by Egyptians in my life; I take them all back by fire, within 24 hours, in the mighty Name of Jesus. (Exod. 15:27)

2. My LORD, make me zealous for You. Keep the Covenant of an everlasting priesthood in my household and descendants forever, in the Name of Jesus. (Num. 25:13)

3. LORD God, let Your hand be upon me and all those that seek me for good. Today, let Your power and Your wrath come against those that are running after my life, in Jesus' Name. (Ezra 8:22)

4. Lord Jesus, forgive me for all my sins that have paralyzed me and brought sickness into my life. Today, replace them all with Your holiness and righteousness, in Jesus' Name. (Matt. 9:2-7, Mark 5:18-25).

5. Lord Jesus, let every one of my garments stand firmly against: every storm, every moth, every fire and every sword of the enemy, as in the days of the three Hebrew children, in the mighty Name of Jesus. (Dan. 3:21)

6. Lord Jesus, the Kingdom of God is like a mustard seed. Architect of my Faith, I decree, every mustard seed you have planted in my destiny, to come forth

now by fire, expanding the kingdom of God, in Jesus' Name. (Matt. 13:31-32, Luke 13:19)

7. Almighty God, I use the key of the house of David to lockup: adultery, fornication, uncleanness, lewdness, idolatry, sorcery, hatred, contentions, jealousies, outburst of wrath (anger), selfishness, ambitions, dissensions, rebellion, heresies, envy, murders, drunkenness, carousing (revelries), evil spirits, excessiveness, factions, gluttony, gossip, greed, hostilities and hypocrisy, in Jesus' Name. (Gal. 5:19-21 Rev. 2:20-22)

8. Lord Jesus, as I partake in your Holy Communion, by eating of Your flesh and drinking of Your blood; heal me in all areas of my life and completely wipe out all sin in my life, in Jesus' Name. (John 6:53)

9. All Sufficient God, incubate and consecrate me with the Holy Ghost like Peter. Ignite me with Your fire, to execute the enemy that lies, deceives and manipulates your Church, in the Name of Jesus. (Acts 5:1-11)

10. Lord God, according to Your Word, let the Spirit of the Lord rest upon me and my family; to promote and proclaim the kingdom of God forever, in the mighty Name of Jesus. (Isa. 11:2-3)

11. Almighty God, separate from me: curses, hexes, spells, bewitchments and any evil domination directed

against me physically and spiritually, in the Name of Jesus. (Zech. 5:7-11, 14:12)

12. Jesus of Nazareth, I remember Your cry and suffering in Gethsemane. Give me the grace to endure through my journey, here on earth, in all areas of my life, in Jesus' Name. (Luke 22:42)

13. Lord Jesus, according to the mysteries in the five loaves of bread and two fish, I receive unspeakable joy in all areas of my life, in Jesus' Name. (Mark 6:34-44)

14. Lord Jesus, because you have died for me, the covenant of death will be annulled and agreement with Sheol will not stand in my life or my descendant's lives, in Jesus' Name. (Isa. 28:18a-c).

15. My God, create in me a clean heart and renew a steadfast spirit within me, in Jesus' Name. (Ps. 51:10)

16. Almighty God, today completely remove any blemishes within me and wash my robes making them white, in the Blood of the Lamb. Lord Jesus, cancel all perverse and crooked hearts, belonging to me and my descendants, in the mighty Name of Jesus. (Deut. 32:5, Rev. 7:14)

17. My Father, I love Jesus. According to Your Word, let me receive the crown of life which You have promised me and my descendants, in Jesus' Name. (Josh. 1:12)

18. The Almighty God, my head will not reject the crown of righteousness which You have laid out for me, in the Name of Jesus. (2 Tim. 4:8)

DAY 11

"Jesus said; "I do not pray for these alone, but also for those who will believe in Me through their word."

John 17:20

Names of Our Lord Jesus Christ:

➤ **Forerunner:** Whither the forerunner is for us entered, even Jesus, made an high priest for ever after the order of Melchizedek. (Hebrews 6:20)

➤ **Glory of the LORD:** And the glory of the LORD shall be revealed, and all flesh shall see it together: for the mouth of the LORD hath spoken it. (Isaiah 40:5)

➤ **God:** The voice of him that cried in the wilderness, prepare ye the way of the LORD, make straight in the desert a highway for our God. (Isaiah 40:3)

Declarations and Confessions:

• I receive the key of the house of David, to open the door of love.

• I receive the key of the house of David, to open the door of praise.

• I receive the key of the house of David, to open the door of obedience.

➤ I receive the key of the house of David, to lockup the door of laziness.

➤ I receive the key of the house of David, to lockup the door to the love of money.

➤ I receive the key of the house of David, to lockup the door of stinginess.

∞ I am complete in Christ. (Colossians 2: 10)

∞ I am confident that the good works God has begun in me will be perfected. (Philippians 1: 5)

❖ **Light of God,** insulate me, incubate me and consecrate me.

❖ **Fire of God,** insulate me, incubate me and consecrate me.

❖ **Blood of Jesus,** insulate me, incubate me and consecrate me.

❖ **Holy Ghost Power,** insulate me, incubate me and consecrate me.

(Scriptures: Gen. 1:3; 1:14, Dan. 3:19-25, 1 Pet. 1:2, Act. 1:8; 2:1-4)

Song of Praises:

Praises, Worship and Thanksgiving (Submit yourself to the Lord)

Prayers:

1. In the name of Jesus, today I denounce and cancel completely, by the Blood of the Lamb, every firstborn (or first-son-syndrome) curse and replace them with the redemptive blessings of the begotten Son, our Lord Jesus Christ. (Luke 2:7)

2. Mighty God, by Your Covenant in the Blood of Jesus Christ, I decree that I completely separate myself, my family and descendants from all satanic activities, in Jesus' Name. (Rev. 12:1)

3. Almighty God of Israel, let Your majestic power, consume every other power that appears to work against my destiny, in Jesus' Name. (Exod. 8:18-19)

4. Lord Jesus, endow me with the gift of faith, like the woman with the issue of blood. Lord, position me to reach Your garment of healing, in every area of my life, in Jesus' Name. (Matt. 9:20-22, Mark 5:25-29)

5. My Father, as You did to Jehoiachin, change every prison garment on me to garments of royalty. Let me continually eat bread from Your table, all the days of my life, in the mighty Name of Jesus. (Jer. 52:33)

6. Lord Jesus, Master of Faith, endow me with Your gift of faith like the mustard seed so that: I will level all mountains and hills; exalt valleys; straighten crooked

roads; and smooth the rough roads; for the expansion of Your Kingdom, in Jesus' Name. (Matt. 13:31-32, Luke 13:19)

7. Almighty God, I use the key of the house of David, to lockup: idolatry, immorality, improvidence, impurity, infirmities, apathy, lack, laziness, love of money and stinginess, in Jesus' Name. (Isa. 22:22)

8. Lord Jesus Christ, though I was once far off from you, I thank you for Your Blood which has brought me near You, in Jesus' Name. (Eph. 2:13)

9. Holy Ghost, this month, I will give birth to my divine destiny helper and divine influence, like You did for Cornelius and Peter. Expand the Kingdom of God upon my life, in Jesus' Name. (Act. 10:1-7)

10. My Father, according to Your Word, let the Spirit of wisdom and understanding rest upon me and my family, to promote and proclaim the Kingdom of God forever, in Jesus' Name. (Isa. 11:2-3)

11. God of Heaven, let all physical and spiritual tests, be converted to testimonies. Let the same be done in: trials to triumphs; failures to successes; scars to stars; bondages to freedom; losses to gains; oppositions to victories; weaknesses to strengths; and negatives to positives, in the mighty Name of Jesus. (Exod. 8:18-19)

12. Jesus of Nazareth, I remember Your crying and suffering in Gethsemane. Give me the heart to forgive those who persecute me, in Jesus' Name. (Luke 15:18-19; 23:34)

13. Almighty God of Israel, according to Your Word, today I pray for the everlasting peace of Jerusalem, in the Name of Jesus. (Ps. 122:6-7)

14. Almighty God of Israel and my Father, according to Your Word, today those who love Jerusalem and their descendants, shall prosper forever, in the Name of Jesus. (Ps. 122:6-7)

15. Almighty God of Israel and my LORD, according to Your Word, today I pray to let the peace from Your throne be within the walls of Jerusalem forever, in the Name of Jesus. (Ps. 122:6-7)

16. Lord Jesus, by the power in Your Blood, I separate from every satanic assignment and activity in my life, in the mighty Name of Jesus. (Rev. 20:10; Matt. 25:41)

17. Almighty God of Israel and my Savior, according to Your Word, today I pray for the peace of Jerusalem forever, in the Name of Jesus. (Ps.122:6-7)

18. Almighty God of Israel and the Alpha and Omega, according to Your Word, today I pray for prosperity within the walls of Jerusalem's palaces forever, in the Name of Jesus. (Ps. 122:6-7)

19. My Father, the Hebrew children received balance in the furnace fire. I receive balance in all areas of my life, my family's life and their descendants, in Jesus' Name. (Dan. 3: 19-25)

20. LORD, I pray O' Lord, those who lead me to captivity, will go into captivity. Those who raise the sword against me, my family and my descendants, shall be killed by the sword, in the mighty Name of Jesus. (Rev. 13:10)

DAY 12

"But we will give ourselves continually to prayer and to the ministry of the word."

Acts 6:4

Names of Our Lord Jesus Christ:

➢ **God Blessed:** Whose are the fathers, and of whom as concerning the flesh Christ came, who is over all, God blessed forever. Amen. (Romans 9:5)

➢ **Good Shepherd:** I am the good shepherd: the good shepherd giveth his life for the sheep. (John 10:11)

➢ **Governor:** And thou Bethlehem, in the land of Judah, art not the least among the princes of Judah: for out of thee shall come a Governor, that shall rule my people Israel. (Matthew 2:6)

Declarations and Confessions:

• I receive the key of the house of David, to open the door of opportunity.

• I receive the key of the house of David, to open the door as an oracle.

• I receive the key of the house of David, to open the door of pastoral gifts.

➢ I receive the key of the house of David, to lockup the door of murder.

➢ I receive the key of the house of David, to lockup the door of anger.

➢ I receive the key of the house of David, to lockup the door of seeking pleasure.

∞ I am hidden with Christ in God. (Colossians 3:3).

∞ I am justified. (Romans 5:1)

❖ **Light of God,** insulate me, incubate me and consecrate me.

❖ **Fire of God,** insulate me, incubate me and consecrate me.

❖ **Blood of Jesus,** insulate me, incubate me and consecrate me.

❖ **Holy Ghost Power,** insulate me, incubate me and consecrate me.

(Scriptures: Gen. 1:3; 1:14, Dan. 3:19-25, 1 Pet. 1:2, Act. 1:8; 2:1-4)

Song of Praises:

Praises, Worship and Thanksgiving (Submit yourself to the Lord)

Prayers:

1. LORD, as You did in the ancient days, let your presence be known to me by: the burning bush, clouds, fire, smoke, rainbow, thunder, lights and wind, in Jesus' Name. (Exod. 3:2; 21; 19: 16; Ezek. 1:4-28; Job 38:1)

2. Lord GOD, inscribe Your Covenant in my heart forever. Today, I reject the image or likeness of anything, which the LORD thy God has forbidden, in the Name of Jesus. (Deut. 4:23)

3. My Lord Jesus Christ, use Your mighty power to teach me Your Word, in the mighty Name of Jesus. (Job 36:22)

4. Lord Jesus, Son of David, open and heal my physical sight to see Your Scriptures; my mental sight to understand Scriptures; and my spiritual sight to see visions, dreams and revelations, in Jesus' Name. (Matt. 9:27-31).

5. LORD, every enemy of my household will wander as a blind man in the streets and their garments shall be polluted, in the Name of Jesus. (Lam. 4:14)

6. Lord Jesus, the kingdom of God is like leaven. Master of Increase, I decree, let increase show in all areas

of my life, in the mighty Name of Jesus. (Matt. 13:33, Luke 13:19)

7. Almighty God, I use the key of the house David, to lockup: murder, anger, hedonism, poverty, powers of darkness, idols, false gods, pride, ridicule, rivalries, selfishness and sexual immorality, in Jesus' Name. (Ps. 49:15)

8. Lord Jesus, though I was once unclean from my birth, I thank You for my re-birth; that has given me the boldness to enter into the holiest, by the Blood of the Lamb, in Jesus' Name. (Heb. 10:19)

9. Almighty God, Peter received new revelation about his ministry at the ninth hour, to meet with Cornelius. Father, let me give birth to new visions, for the expansion of the Kingdom of God, in Jesus' Name. (Acts 10:1-7)

10. Lord GOD, according to Your Word, let the Spirit of counsel, power and might rest upon me and my family, in order to promote and proclaim the Kingdom of God forever, in Jesus' Name. (Isa. 11:2-3)

11. Father, by the power in Your Blood, separate and cleanse me from every infirmity introduced into my life. I command those ungodly powers to receive Holy Ghost fire now, in the Name of Jesus. (Acts 3:1-10)

12. Lord GOD, I thank You because You always hear me. Display Your glory upon my life and let every dead thing receive life, restoration and resurrection power, in Jesus' Name. (John 11:41-43)

13. Almighty God of Israel, according to Your Word, today I pray for my family and my church. Let peace reign forever for me and my descendants, in the Name of Jesus. (Ps. 122:6-7)

14. Almighty God of Israel and my Majestic King, according to Your Word, those who love me and their descendants, shall prosper in their land forever, in the Name of Jesus. (Ps.122:6-7)

15. Almighty God of Israel and my incredible Master, according to Your Word, let peace abound in every wall of my life, in the Name of Jesus. (Ps. 122:6-7)

16. Almighty God of Israel and my inconceivable Comforter, according to Your Word, build prosperity within my palace for Your glory forever, in the Name of Jesus. (Ps. 122:6-7)

17. Almighty God of Israel and my Lord, according to Your Word, today I pray let peace from Your throne be within the walls of Jerusalem forever, in the Name of Jesus. (Ps.122:6-7)

18. King of kings and Lord of lords, let the Spirit of the Lord come upon me. Anoint me to preach the gospel

to the poor and to heal the brokenhearted, in the mighty Name of Jesus. (Luke 6:18-19)

DAY 13

"Likewise the Spirit also helps in our weakness. For we do not know what should pray for as we ought, but the Spirit Himself makes intercession for us with groanings which cannot be uttered."

Romans 8:26

Names of Our Lord Jesus Christ:

> ➢ **Great High Priest:** Seeing then that we have a great high priest, that is passed into the heavens, Jesus the Son of God, let us hold fast our profession. (Hebrews 4:14)
>
> ➢ **Head of the Church:** And hath put all things under his feet, and gave him to be the head over all things to the church. (Ephesians 1:22)
>
> ➢ **Head of all things:** Hath in these last days spoken unto us by his Son, whom he hath appointed heir of all things, by whom also he made the worlds. (Hebrews 1:2)

Declarations and Confessions:

- I receive the key of the house of David, to open the door of patience.
- I receive the key of the house of David, to open the door of peace.
- I receive the key of the house of David, to open the door of supernatural power.

> ➢ I receive the key of the house of David, to lock up the door of poverty.
>
> ➢ I receive the key of the house of David, to lock up the door to the power of darkness.

➤ I receive the key of the house of David, to lock up the door of pride.

∞ I am God's co-worker. (1 Corinth. 3:9; 2 Corinthians 6:1)

∞ I am God's workmanship. (Ephesians 2:10)

❖ **Light of God,** insulate me, incubate me and consecrate me.

❖ **Fire of God,** insulate me, incubate me and consecrate me.

❖ **Blood of Jesus,** insulate me, incubate me and consecrate me.

❖ **Holy Ghost Power,** insulate me, incubate me and consecrate me.

(Scriptures: Gen. 1:3; 1:14, Dan. 3:19-25, 1 Pet. 1:2, Act. 1:8; 2:1-4)

Song of Praises:

Praises, Worship and Thanksgiving (Submit yourself to the Lord)

Prayers:

1. Lord God, Your Covenant of Salt that you established with David forever; have it remain in my life permanently and in the lives of my descendants, in Jesus' Name. (2 Chron. 13:5; Mark 9:49).

2. My LORD God, You are God, the faithful God, who keeps covenant and mercy. Do not let me depart from Your love and Your commandments, in Jesus' Name. (Deut. 7:9)

3. LORD, receive me by Your mighty power. Redeem my soul from the power of: the grave, shame, illness, lack, poverty, idols and other false gods, in the Name of Jesus. (Ps. 49:15)

4. Son of David, I believe and I have faith in You. From today onward, fill my mouth and my tongue with testimonies of Your miracle healing power, in all areas of my life, in Jesus' Name. (Matt 9:27-31)

5. Father and Lord Jesus, remove my stolen garments of honor from my enemy's house and return them back to my house by fire, in Jesus' Name. (Num. 20:26-28)

6. Lord Jesus and Master of Multiplication, the kingdom of God is like yeast. Spirit of yeast, come forth now to my destiny and multiply in all areas of my life, in the mighty Name of Jesus. (Matt. 13:33, Luke 13:19-21)

7. Almighty, I use the key of David to lockup: shame, sickness, slander, slovenliness, sorcery, strife, drunkenness, stubbornness, uncontrolled habits, food from idols, gods, unwise speech and worldly worship, in Jesus' Name. (Exod. 8:18-19)

8. Lord Jesus, the Mediator of the New Covenant and to the Blood sprinkling; let Your Blood speak better things in my life and my family's life, than that of Abel, in Jesus' Name. (Heb. 12:24)

9. My Lord, I pray, let my offerings and sacrifices come up for memorial before you, in Jesus' Name. (Act. 10:1-6; Gen. 4:3-4)

10. Lord GOD, according to Your Word, let the Spirit of knowledge and fear of God, rest upon me and my family, to promote and proclaim the Kingdom of God forever, in Jesus' Name. (Isa. 112:3)

11. Almighty God, I reject by fire every son of perdition and power of darkness, assigned to prevent me from doing Your work, in Jesus' Name. (John 17:12)

12. Lord GOD, I thank You because You always hear me. Glorify Your name upon my life, in every challenge and obstacle, in Jesus' Name. (John 12:27-28)

13. My Lord, today I decree my light will shine in the darkness and the darkness will not comprehend it, in the Name of Jesus. (John 1:5)

14. O Lord, in my life, every spirit of manipulation and deception of satan working through dreams and visions, receive the fire of God. Today, I nullify their activities permanently, by the Blood of Jesus, in the mighty Name of Jesus. (Matt. 4:6, Ps. 91:12)

15. Father, according to Your Word; I decree my sons and daughters shall prophesy, my old man shall dream dreams, and my young man shall see visions, in the Name of Jesus. (Joel 2:28)

16. Lord Jesus, anything resembling Lazarus' death in my life, receive the resurrection power of Christ, for my breakthrough and my descendants' breakthrough, in Jesus' Name. (John 11:1-44)

17. Lord Jesus, anything resembling Lazarus' stone in my life, be rolled away and receive the resurrection power of Christ, for my breakthrough and my descendants' breakthrough, in Jesus' Name. (John 11:1-44)

18. Lord Jesus, anything resembling Lazarus' decaying body in my life, be revived and receive the resurrection power of Christ for my breakthrough and my descendants' breakthrough, in Jesus' Name. (John 11:1-44)

DAY 14

"Rejoicing in hope, patient in tribulation, continuing steadfastly in prayer."

Romans 12:12

Names of Our Lord Jesus Christ:

➤ **Holy Child:** For of a truth against thy holy child Jesus, whom thou hast anointed, both Herod, and Pontius Pilate, with the Gentiles, and the people of Israel, were gathered together. (Acts 4:27)

➤ **Holy One:** But ye denied the Holy One and the Just, and desired a murderer to be granted unto you. (Acts 3:14)

➤ **Holy One of God:** Saying, Let us alone; what have we to do with thee, thou Jesus of Nazareth? art thou come to destroy us? I know thee who thou art, the Holy One of God. (Mark 1:24)

Declarations and Confessions:

• I receive the key of the house of David, to open the door of prophetic gifts.

• I receive the key of the house of David, to open the door of prosperity.

• I receive the key of the house of David, to open the door of Scriptures.

➤ I receive the key of the house of David, to lockup the door of ridicule.

➤ I receive the key of the house of David, to lockup the door of selfish rivalry.

➢ I receive the key of the house of David, to lockup the door of selfishness.

∞ I have been redeemed and forgiven. (Colossians 1:14).

∞ I have been adopted as God's child. (Ephesians 1:5)

❖ **Light of God,** insulate me, incubate me and consecrate me.

❖ **Fire of God,** insulate me, incubate me and consecrate me.

❖ **Blood of Jesus,** insulate me, incubate me and consecrate me.

❖ **Holy Ghost Power,** insulate me, incubate me and consecrate me.

(Scriptures: Gen. 1:3; 1:14, Dan. 3:19-25, 1 Pet. 1:2, Act. 1:8; 2:1-4)

Song of Praises:

Praises, Worship and Thanksgiving (Submit yourself to the Lord)

Prayers:

1. Lord, let Your ear be attentive to me, as Your son and grant me mercy in the presence of all people, in Jesus' Name. (Neh. 1:4-11)

2. Father, all foolishness in my life that could break Your covenant with me or not allow Your covenant to be established in my life; I decree, that all foolishness will catch fire and burn, in Jesus' Name. (Deut. 31: 16-20)

3. God you have spoken once, twice, and have I heard that power belongs unto You, God. Every spoken Word, through my dreams, visions and revelations concerning my destiny, let them manifest now, in the mighty Name of Jesus. (Luke 2:25-32)

4. The Mighty Healer, Lord Jesus, give me the gift of prayer and fasting; to heal the dumb to speak, the deaf to hear, and the demon possessed to be set free, in the mighty Name of Jesus. (Matt. 9:32-33; Mark 7:24-30)

5. Every evil deceit of the Gibeonites regarding my destiny, today be exposed and receive permanent shame in their shoes and garments. I decree their bread of provision shall be dried up and molded, in Jesus' Name. (Josh. 9:4-5)

6. Jesus, the kingdom of God is like hidden treasure in a field. Christ my Treasure, take from me, by fire, all things appearing in this world that seek to take or replace the Kingdom in me, in Jesus' Name. (Matt. 13:44)

7. Lion of Judah, as You did to Eglon, king of Moab, I use the sword of heaven to destroy my enemies. I lock them up with Your heavenly key and see them fallen down dead, in Jesus' Name. (Judg. 3:19-30)

8. Jesus, sanctify me and my family with Your Blood, which suffered without the gate. Endow me with Your strength, in the mighty Name of Jesus. (Heb. 13:12-14)

9. All Sufficient God, insulate, incubate and consecrate me with the power of the Holy Ghost, like You did to Paul and Silas. Let every prison wall that surrounds me collapse today, in Jesus' Name. (Acts 15:25-40)

10. Almighty God, I reject all counterfeit and evil: friends, alliances, family, husband, wife, children, marriage, engagements, trading, pursuit, ornaments, money, relatives, business and ministry, in the mighty Name of Jesus. (Josh. 9:16-27)

11. Lord GOD, I thank You because You always hear me. Keep unity among the nations, churches, all believers and their families, in the mighty Name of Jesus. (John 17:1-end)

12. Lord Jesus, anything resembling or representing Lazarus' death and garments of death and sorrow, now loose from me completely. I receive the resurrection power of Christ Jesus, in all areas of my life and my descendants' lives, in Jesus' Name. (John 11:44)

13. Lord Jesus, anything resembling or representing Lazarus' death and the stone of trouble and tribulation, now roll away from me completely. I receive the full resurrection power of Christ Jesus, in all areas of my life and my descendants' lives, in Jesus' Name. (John 11:39)

14. Lord Jesus, anything resembling or representing Lazarus' death and the mind-set of the earthly body, change me to the mind-set of heaven. I receive the resurrection power of Christ Jesus, in all areas of my life and my descendants' lives, in Jesus' Name. (John 11:39; 1Corinth. 5:1)

15. Jesus of Nazareth, every one of my promotions in ministry, business and career, residing in the enemy's hands, receive Holy Ghost fire, today. I redirect them to my house now, in the Name of Jesus. (Exod. 8:18-19)

16. O Mighty God, every evil spirit truncating my job, ministry, business and my destiny, receive the fire of God today, in Jesus' Name. (Zech 14:12)

17. Holy Ghost and fire, consume every idol holding my blessings. I receive Your abundant blessings, in the Name of Jesus. (Ps. 129:8)

18. Lord Jesus, cleanse my heart and my garments to worship You, in purity and in holiness, every day of my life, in the Name of Jesus. (Rev. 2:5)

19. Lord Jesus, cleanse me inside and out. Purify me to praise You forever, in Jesus' Name. (Rev. 2:5)

DAY 15

"Do not deprive one another except with consent for a time, that you may give yourselves to fasting and prayer; and come together again so that satan does not tempt you because of your lack of self-control."

1 Corinthians 7:5

Names of Our Lord Jesus Christ:

> **Holy One of Israel:** Fear not, thou worm Jacob, and ye men of Israel; I will help thee, saith the LORD, and thy redeemer, the Holy One of Israel. (Isaiah 41:14)

> **Horn of Salvation:** And hath raised up an horn of salvation for us in the house of his servant David. (Luke 1:69)

> **I am:** Jesus said unto them, Verily, verily, I say unto you, before Abraham was, I am. (John 8:58)

Declarations and Confessions:

- I receive the key of the house of David, to open the door to see God.
- I receive the key of the house of David, to open the door of self control.
- I receive the key of the house of David, to open the door of service to God.

> I receive the key of the house of David, to lockup the door of sexual immorality.

> I receive the key of the house of David, to lockup the door of shame.

> I receive the key of the house of David, to lockup the door of sickness.

∞ I am predestined to be adopted. (Ephesians 1:5)

∞ I am a child of God. (1 John 3:1)

❖ **Light of God,** insulate me, incubate me and consecrate me.

❖ **Fire of God,** insulate me, incubate me and consecrate me.

❖ **Blood of Jesus,** insulate me, incubate me and consecrate me.

❖ **Holy Ghost Power,** insulate me, incubate me and consecrate me.

(Scriptures: Gen. 1:3; 1:14, Dan. 3:19-25, 1 Pet. 1:2, Act. 1:8; 2:1-4)

Song of Praises:

Praises, Worship and Thanksgiving (Submit yourself to the Lord)

Prayers:

1. Lord GOD, according to Your Word, let Your Kingdom come, in my life. I pray O' Lord, let my eyes see the invisible and let my ears hear the inaudible (voice of God). My Father, let my feet level mountains, straighten the crooked road, smooth the rough road and exalt the valleys, in Jesus' Name. (Matt 6:9; Isa. 40:4-5)

2. Almighty God, by the New Covenant and in the name of Jesus Christ, every knee shall bow. I decree in the mighty Name of Jesus, every Egyptian and King Herod in my destiny, be consumed by the fire of the Holy Ghost now, in Jesus' Name. (Isa. 45:23)

3. LORD, I denounce and cancel every spirit of sorcery, connected to me and my ancestors, by the power in the Blood of the Lamb, in Jesus' Name. (Exod. 22:18)

4. Father, how great are Your works. Equip me through the greatness of Your power, that cannot be disgraced. Make my enemies be subdued under my feet, in the Name of Jesus. (Ps. 66:3)

5. The Great Physician, heal my head, hands and legs. Uproot everything planted in my body contrary to the will of God. Make me fruitful for Your Kingdom, in Jesus' Name. (Matt. 12:10-13)

6. Lord Jesus Christ, send my destiny helper to me. Jonathan stripped himself of his garments for David. I receive all my garments: sword, bow and girdle of honor, from my destiny helper, in Jesus' Name. (1 Sam. 18:4)

7. Lord Jesus, You are my hidden treasure. I forsake this world treasure for Your precious treasure, in the mighty Name of Jesus. (Matt. 13:44)

8. LORD, the Son of David, use the key of the house of David, on your shoulder; to open doors no one shall shut and shut doors that no one shall open in my life, in Jesus' Name. (Isa. 22: 22)

9. Almighty God of Peace, that raised our Lord Jesus Christ from the dead. The Great Shepherd of the sheep, through Your Blood, let Your everlasting Covenant remain with me forever, in Jesus' Name. (Heb. 13:20)

10. Lord Jesus, as You did to the lame man at the ninth hour of prayer, at the gate called beautiful; let everything that is crippled in my life, receive strength now, in the mighty Name of Jesus. (Act. 3:1-10)

11. King of kings and Lord of lords, let the Spirit of the Lord be upon me. Anoint me to preach the gospel, proclaim liberty to the captives and recover sight to the blind, in the mighty Name of Jesus. (Luke 4:18-19)

12. Lord Jesus, let Your Kingdom come upon me. Let my spiritual eyes see the invisible, let my ears hear the inaudible (voice of God) and let my mouth speak like an oracle of God, in the precious Name of Jesus. (Luke 24:30-31)

13. Our Father in heaven, hallowed be Your name. Let Your Kingdom come upon my life and all circumstances, related to my destiny on earth, in Jesus' Name. (John 1:46-51)

14. My Father, the Hebrew children received balance in the furnace fire. I receive balance in all areas of my finances, in the mighty Name of Jesus. (Dan. 3:19-25)

15. My Father, the Hebrew children received balance in the furnace fire. I receive balance in every area of the Spirit of the LORD: Spirit of God rest upon me, Spirit of wisdom, Spirit of understanding, Spirit of counsel, Spirit of might, Spirit of knowledge, and the Spirit of the fear of the LORD, in the mighty Name of Jesus. (Dan,3:19-25; Isa. 11:2)

16. My Father, the Hebrew children received balance in the furnace fire. I receive balance in all areas of my career, in the mighty Name of Jesus. (Dan. 3:19-25)

17. My Father, the Hebrew children received balance in the furnace fire. I receive balance in all areas of my health, in the mighty Name of Jesus. (Dan. 3:19-25)

18. My Father, the Hebrew children received balance in the furnace fire. I receive balance in every area of my anointing, in the mighty Name of Jesus. (Dan. 3:19-25)

19. My Father, the Hebrew children received balance in the furnace fire. I receive balance in every area of my calling and purpose, in the mighty Name of Jesus. (Dan. 3:19-25)

20. My Father, the Hebrew children received balance in the furnace fire. I receive balance in every area of my ministry, in the mighty Name of Jesus.

(Dan. 3: 19-25)

DAY 16

"For if I pray in a tongue, my spirit prays, but my understanding is unfruitful. What is the conclusion then? I
will pray with the spirit, and I will also pray with understanding. I will sing with the spirit, and I will also sing
with the understanding."

1 Corinthians 14:14-15

Names of Our Lord Jesus Christ:

- ➤ **Image of God:** In whom the god of this world hath blinded the minds of them which believe not, lest the light of the glorious gospel of Christ, who is the image of God, should shine unto them. (2 Corinthians 4:4)
- ➤ **Immanuel:** Therefore the Lord himself shall give you a sign; Behold, a virgin shall conceive, and bear a son, and shall call his name Immanuel. (Isaiah 7:14)
- ➤ **Jehovah:** Trust ye in the LORD for ever: for in the LORD JEHOVAH is everlasting strength. (Isaiah 26:4)

Declarations and Confessions:

- • I receive the key of the house of David, to open the door of service to God.
- • I receive the key of the house of David, to open the door to the aroma of God.
- • I receive the key of the house of David, to open the door to the gift of teaching.

- ➤ I receive the key of the house of David, to lockup the door of slander.
- ➤ I receive the key of the house of David, to lockup the door of slovenliness.
- ➤ I receive the key of the house of David, to lockup the door of sorcery.

∞ I am precious to God. (Isaiah 43:4)

∞ I am called by my name. (Isaiah 43:1)

❖ **Light of God,** insulate me, incubate me and consecrate me.

❖ **Fire of God,** insulate me, incubate me and consecrate me.

❖ **Blood of Jesus,** insulate me, incubate me and consecrate me.

❖ **Holy Ghost Power,** insulate me, incubate me and consecrate me.

(Scriptures: Gen. 1:3; 1:14, Dan. 3:19-25, 1 Pet. 1:2, Act. 1:8; 2:1-4)

Song of Praises:

Praises, Worship and Thanksgiving (Submit yourself to the Lord)

Prayers:

1. LORD God, grant Your Word in my heart, like a burning fire shut up in my bones, in the mighty Name of Jesus. (Jer. 20:9)

2. God, I refuse to transgress the covenant of the LORD my God and I pronounce that I will not serve or bow down to other gods. My descendants and I will enjoy the full covenant of God, in Jesus' Name. (Josh. 23:16)

3. God, the Ancients of Days, forsake me not when I am old and have gray hair. Let me show Your strength and power to this generation and beyond, in Jesus' Name. (Ps. 71: 18)

4. Lord Jesus, with Your precious Blood, anoint me with Your great power to destroy the spirit of blindness, deafness and dumbness and to proclaim the Name of Jesus, in His mighty Name. (Matt. 12:22, Mark 7:31-37)

5. Lord my God, wipe out with Your precious blood, all strange gods and idols around me, today. Cleanse me and change my garments, in the Name of Jesus. (Gen. 35:2)

6. Lord, the kingdom of God is like a merchant, seeking beautiful pearls. Master of accretion, perfect me as

Your true Church, for the presentation and fulfillment of Your mystery, in Jesus' Name. (Matt. 13:45-46)

7. Lord Jesus, woe to lawyers in my life that have taken the key of knowledge away from me. I take back by fire, every key of knowledge the enemy has taken from me, in Jesus' Name. (Luke 11:52)

8. Lord Jesus, according to your Word: through sanctification of the Spirit, obedience and Your blood; let grace and peace be multiplied in my life forever, in Jesus' Name. (1 Peter 1:2)

9. God Almighty, like You did to Peter at the ninth hour, let every utterance proceeding out of my mouth bring: healing, deliverance, unspeakable joy and uplift nations, in Jesus' Name. (Acts 10:1-6)

10. King of kings and Lord of lords, let the Spirit of the Lord be upon me. Anoint me to preach the gospel and to set at liberty those who are oppressed and to proclaim the acceptable year of the LORD, in the mighty Name of Jesus. (Luke 4:18-19)

11. Almighty God, today I decree and invoke, according to Your Scripture in Psalm 91, let these covenantal prayers work for me and my descendants, in Jesus' Name. (Ps. 91)

12. Father, the God who answers by fire; answer my prayers by fire whenever there's a spiritual attack against me, in the mighty Name of Jesus. (Ps. 91)

13. My Lord Jesus, teach me, instruct me and direct me to the place of my destiny with You. Let Your grace abide with me forever, to listen and obey You, in all areas of my life, in Jesus' Name. (Acts 9:6-11)

14. My Father, the Hebrew children received balance in the furnace fire. I receive balance in all areas of my giving to the house of God, in the mighty Name of Jesus. (Dan. 3:20-25)

15. My Father, the Hebrew children received balance in the furnace fire. I receive balance in all areas of my spiritual gifts, in the mighty Name of Jesus. (Dan. 3:20-25)

16. My Father, the Hebrew children received balance in the furnace fire. I receive balance in all areas of my spiritual growth, in the mighty Name of Jesus. (Dan. 3:20-25)

17. My Father, the Hebrew children received balance in the furnace fire. I receive balance in all areas of my spiritual power, in the mighty Name of Jesus. (Dan. 3:20-25)

18. My Father, the Hebrew children received balance in the furnace fire. I receive balance in all areas of my

spiritual healing, in the mighty Name of Jesus. (Dan. 3:20-25)

DAY 17

"Praying always with all prayer and supplication in the Spirit, being watchful to this end with all perseverance and supplication for all saints and for me, that utterance may be given to me, that I may open my mouth boldly to make know the mystery of the gospel."

Ephesians 6:18-19

Names of Our Lord Jesus Christ:

➢ **Jesus:** And she shall bring forth a son, and thou shalt call his name JESUS: for he shall save his people from their sins. (Matthew 1:21)

➢ **Jesus of Nazareth:** And the multitude said, This is Jesus the prophet of Nazareth of Galilee. (Matthew 21:11)

➢ **Judge of Israel:** Now gather thyself in troops, O daughter of troops: he hath laid siege against us: they shall smite the judge of Israel with a rod upon the cheek. (Micah 5:1)

Declarations and Confessions:

• I receive the key of the house of David, to open the door of understanding.

• I receive the key of the house of David, to open the door of walking with God.

• I receive the key of the house of David, to open the door of supernatural wealth.

➢ I receive the key of the house of David, to lockup the door of strife.

➢ I receive the key of the house of David, to lockup the door of drunkenness.

➢ I receive the key of the house of David, to lock up the door of stubbornness.

∞ I am accepted by God. (Ephesians 1:6)

∞ I am baptized with Christ. (Romans 6:4)

❖ **Light of God,** insulate me, incubate me and consecrate me.

❖ **Fire of God,** insulate me, incubate me and consecrate me.

❖ **Blood of Jesus,** insulate me, incubate me and consecrate me.

❖ **Holy Ghost Power,** insulate me, incubate me and consecrate me.

(Scriptures: Gen. 1:3; 1:14, Dan. 3:19-25, 1 Pet. 1:2, Act. 1:8; 2:1-4)

Song of Praises:

Praises, Worship and Thanksgiving (Submit yourself to the Lord)

Prayers:

1. Almighty God, make me lie down in green pastures and lead me beside still waters, in the mighty Name of Jesus. (Ps. 23:2.)

2. LORD God of Israel, there is no God like You, in heaven above or on earth. My Father who keeps covenant, have mercy on me, my family and my descendants, in Jesus' Name. (1 Kings 8:23)

3. Almighty God of heaven, endow me with Your riches, wealth and honor. I thank You for the power to eat of it, receive my portion and rejoice in my labor, in the Name of Jesus. (Eccl. 5:19)

4. Almighty God, I have victory over every sickness that has crippled my: job, business, health, ministry, finances and family, by the power of the Holy Ghost, in the mighty Name of Jesus. (Acts 1:1-8)

5. Lord Jesus Christ, clothe me with Your holy garments. Anoint me and sanctify me to minister Your Word, each day of my life, in Jesus' Name. (Exod. 40:13)

6. King of kings and Master of Perfection, perfect me and make me worthy as one of Your children. Baptize me by one Spirit into the Body of Christ, in the mighty Name of Jesus. (Matt. 13:45-46, 1 Corinth. 12:12-13)

7. LORD of Hosts, with Your sword; pursue, punish and destroy: the fleeing leviathan serpent, the flying leviathan serpent, the twisted leviathan serpent and the reptile of the sea. All serpents challenging the kingdom of God upon my life and my descendants' lives, cut them all into pieces, in the mighty Name of Jesus. (Isa. 14:29; 27:1, Zech. 5:5-11;14:12)

8. Lord Jesus, my Savior and the One that lives, was once dead and behold is alive for evermore. Today lockup hell and death in my life permanently, in Jesus' Name. (Rev. 1:18)

9. My God, the God of Light, let me walk in Your light and fellowship with You. Let the Blood of Your Son, Jesus Christ, cleanse me from all sin, in the mighty Name of Jesus. (1 John 1:7)

10. Lord God in Heaven, today I decree that I give birth to nations inside me. They shall walk, leap, and praise the Holy God in the Highest, in Jesus' Name. (Acts 3:1-10)

11. Almighty God, from today onward, I will share Your Word as a prophet and not as a story-teller, in the mighty Name of Jesus. (Dan. 3:27-29; Hosea 12:13)

12. Lord Jesus, replace all satanic dreams in my life with heavenly visions and divinely-inspired dreams, in Jesus' Name. (Dan. 7:1-22; Rev. 1:8-11)

13. My Father, grant me Your quick discernment and the willing Spirit of intercession in prayer for churches, believers and unbelievers, in mighty Name of Jesus. (Eph. 1:17-20, 3:14-21; 6:18-20, Heb. 13:20-21)

14. Mighty God, as You did to Pharaoh in Egypt, Father, do not harden my heart towards evil. Change my heart of stone to a heart of flesh, in the Name of Jesus. (Heb. 3:8, 15)

15. Father, remove all unrighteousness from me, completely. Today, I receive righteousness and inherit the Kingdom of God forever, in the mighty Name of Jesus. (1 Corinth. 6:9)

16. Ancient of Days, let the Word of Christ dwell in me richly in all wisdom; teaching and admonishing one in another in psalms, hymns and spiritual songs, singing with grace in my heart to my Lord, in Jesus' Name. (Col. 3:16)

17. My Father, the Hebrew children received balance in the furnace fire. I receive balance in all areas of spiritual wealth, in the mighty Name of Jesus. (Dan. 3:25)

18. The Holy One of Israel, cover me with Your garment of holiness, in the mighty Name of Jesus. (Rev. 3:5)

19. Father, I will eat the unleavened bread of Your temple and I shall appear in Your sacred place, in the Name of Jesus. (Exod. 12:15-20)

20. Lord Jesus, according to Your Names: **Wonderful, Counselor, Mighty God, Everlasting Father, Prince of Peace**, let these names begin to work for me in all areas of my life, in Jesus' Name. (Isa. 9:6)

DAY 18

"Be anxious for nothing, but in everything by prayer and supplication, with thanksgiving, let your request be made know to God; and the peace of God which surpassed all understanding, will guard your hearts and minds through Christ Jesus."

Philippians 4:6-7

Names of Our Lord Jesus Christ:

> **The Just One:** Which of the prophets have not your fathers persecuted? and they have slain them which showed before of the coming of the Just One; of whom ye have been now the betrayers and murderers. (Acts 7:52)

> **King:** Rejoice greatly, O daughter of Zion; shout, O daughter of Jerusalem: behold, thy King cometh unto thee: he is just, and having salvation; lowly, and riding upon an ass, and upon a colt the foal of an ass. (Zechariah 9:9)

> **King of the Ages:** Now unto the King eternal, immortal, invisible, the only wise God, be honor and glory forever and ever. Amen. (1 Timothy 1:17)

Declarations and Confessions:

- I receive the key of the house of David, to open the door of wisdom.
- I receive the key of the house of David, to open the door of the Word of God.
- I receive the key of the house of David, to open the door to worshipping the Creator.

> I receive the key of the house of David, to lockup the door of uncontrolled habits.

➢ I receive the key of the house of David, to lockup the door of unwise speech.

➢ I receive the key of the house of David, to lockup the door of worldly worship.

∞ I am hidden with Christ. (Psalms 32:7)

∞ I am chosen. (Ephesians 1:4)

❖ **Light of God,** insulate me, incubate me and consecrate me.

❖ **Fire of God,** insulate me, incubate me and consecrate me.

❖ **Blood of Jesus,** insulate me, incubate me and consecrate me.

❖ **Holy Ghost Power,** insulate me, incubate me and consecrate me.

(Scriptures: Gen. 1:3; 1:14, Dan. 3:19-25, 1 Pet. 1:2, Act. 1:8; 2:1-4)

Song of Praises:

Praises, Worship and Thanksgiving (Submit yourself to the Lord)

Prayers:

1. Jehovah God, plant me like a tree by the waters, spreading out her roots by the river and shall not cease during drought. My leaves shall remain green and yield fruit forever, in Jesus' Name. (Ps. 1:3, Jer. 17: 8, Rev. 22:1-2)

2. Almighty God, through the Blood Covenant of Jesus Christ, let the Blood work today for me, my family, my children and their descendants, in the Name of Jesus. (1 John 1:7)

3. My Lord GOD, who made heaven and earth by His wisdom and power; stretch out Your arm today and rescue me from the calamity of this world, in the Name of Jesus. (Jer. 32:17)

4. Almighty God and by Your Blood, I destroy and have victory over: lameness, blindness, deafness, dumbness, fear and hemorrhages, in the mighty Name of Jesus. (1 Pet. 1:2)

5. Almighty God and by Your Blood, I destroy and have victory over: dropsy, leprosy, slavery, epilepsy, unclean spirits, sickness, poverty, lack, illness and unfruitfulness, by the power of the Holy Ghost, in Jesus' Name. (Mark 11:12-24)

6. Lord Jesus Christ, as the woman with the issue of blood touched the hem of Your garment and received healing, anoint my garments as a source of healing, for all diseases and sicknesses, in Jesus' Name. (Matt. 26:28)

7. Lord Jesus, the Kingdom of God is like a net cast into the sea. Master Jesus, gather me as one of Your good vessels and my salvation will remain in your Kingdom forever, in Jesus' Name. (Matt. 13:47-48)

8. Lord Jesus, the beholder of the key of the house of David, laid upon Your shoulder. Use the key to open which no man can shut, and shut which no man can open in my life, in Jesus' Name. (Rev. 3:7, Isa. 22:22)

9. Mighty One of Israel who came by Water and Blood; Jesus Christ, separate me from the world with Your precious Blood to overcome an earthly mind and direct me to the Spirit of truth, in Jesus' Name. (1 John 5:6; John 17)

10. Almighty God, I pray every evil tree planted on the journey of my life, be uprooted now and burn in the lake of fire, permanently. I will not see them again, in Jesus Name. (Mark 11:12-24)

11. Almighty God, equip and endow me with all Your spiritual gifts: administration, apostleship, prophecy, encouragement, evangelism, faith, prayer, giving, ser-

vice, knowledge, leadership, mercy, preaching, pastoring, teaching, wisdom, miracles, healing, tongues, interpretation of tongues, in the mighty Name of Jesus. (1 Corinth. 12:8-11)

12. Almighty God of Heaven, I use Your key and padlock of heaven to lockup: tragedy, sorrow, lack, shame, poverty, idols, false gods, initiations, disappointment and failure in my life, in Jesus' Name. (Isa. 22.22, Rev. 3:7)

13. Father, You remembered Cornelius at the ninth hour of prayer and the penitent thief at the cross. Lord, please remember me in all areas of my life, in Jesus' Name. (Luke 23:42, 15:18-19)

14. My Heavenly Father, I thank You because You always heard my prayers. Today, I receive answers to all the prayers I have prayed in my life, in Jesus' Name. (John 15:8)

15. Father, today I receive the power to make wealth. My Lord, appear suddenly in all my situations, in the Name of Jesus. (Deut. 8:18)

16. My Lord Jesus Christ, work with me and confirm Your Word with me as I preach the gospel to the nations. Let signs and wonders follow me just as You commissioned the eleven apostles, in Jesus' Name. (Mark 16:15-20)

17. Lord God of Israel, from the beginning of the year to the end, let Your eyes remain on me and all that concerns me and my descendants, in Jesus' Name. (Deut. 1:11; 11:12, Ps.91)

18. Ancient of Days, let my eyes and feet work together constantly, to glorify the Kingdom of God, in the mighty Name of Jesus. (Job 29:15, Ps. 25:15.116:18)

19. LORD of Hosts, with Your sword; pursue, punish and destroy: the fleeing leviathan serpent, the flying leviathan serpent, the twisted leviathan serpent and the reptile of the sea. All serpents challenging the kingdom of God upon my life and my descendants' lives, cut them all into pieces, in the mighty Name of Jesus. (Isa. 14:29; 27:1, Zech. 5:5-11; 14:12)

DAY 19

"Epaphras, who is one of you, a bondservant of Christ, greets you, always laboring fervently for you in prayers, that you may stand perfect and complete in all the will of God."

Colossians 4:12

Names of Our Lord Jesus Christ:

- ➤ **King of the Jews:** Saying, Where is he that is born King of the Jews? for we have seen his star in the east, and are come to worship him. (Matthew 2:2)
- ➤ **King of Kings:** Which in his times he shall show, who is the blessed and only Potentate, the King of kings, and Lord of lords. (1 Timothy 6:15)
- ➤ **King of Saints:** And they sing the song of Moses the servant of God, and the song of the Lamb, saying, Great and marvelous are thy works, Lord God Almighty; just and true are thy ways, thou King of saints. (Revelation 15:3)

Declarations and Confessions:

- I receive the key of the house of David, to open the door of perpetual power.
- I receive the key of the house of David, to open the door of prophetic prayer.
- I receive the key of the house of David, to open the door of the prophetic office.

- ➤ I receive the key of the house of David, to lockup the door of satanic dreams.
- ➤ I receive the key of the house of David, to lockup the door to filthy imaginations.

➢ I receive the key of the house of David, to lockup the door of filthy conversations.

∞ I am born again. (John 3:7)

∞ I am saved. (Ephesians 2:8)

❖ **Light of God,** insulate me, incubate me and consecrate me.

❖ **Fire of God,** insulate me, incubate me and consecrate me.

❖ **Blood of Jesus,** insulate me, incubate me and consecrate me.

❖ **Holy Ghost Power,** insulate me, incubate me and consecrate me.

(Scriptures: Gen. 1:3; 1:14, Dan. 3:19-25, 1 Pet. 1:2, Act. 1:8; 2:1-4)

Song of Praises:

Praises, Worship and Thanksgiving (Submit yourself to the Lord)

Prayers:

1. My LORD, as I minister Your Word, grant Your Word into my mouth like liquid fire, that breaks rock into pieces, in the mighty Name of Jesus. (Jer. 23:29)

2. God of Israel, Your covenant remains in my life forever. I will not fear other gods, nor bow to them, nor serve them, nor sacrifice to them, nor eat their delicacies, in Jesus' Name. (2 Kings 17:35)

3. Almighty God and my Great Warrior, endow me with Your power, strength and glory to: level mountains, exalt valleys, straighten crooked roads and smooth the rough roads, in Jesus' Name. (Dan. 2:37, 1 Pet. 5:10)

4. Lord Jesus, in the land of the living, my family and I will not experience any of the Egyptian diseases or plagues, because of Your precious Blood, in Jesus' Name. (Exod. 7:14-25; 8; 9;10; 11)

5. Lord Jesus, awake and strengthen me O Zion! Clothe me with Your beautiful garments, O Jerusalem, the Holy City. Father, separate me from unclean garments and unclean spirits, in Jesus' Name. (Rev. 2:18-22; 3:4-5)

6. Lord Jesus and Master of my salvation, do not cast me into the furnace fire, yet make me one of Your

good vessels for the Kingdom of God, in Jesus' Name. (Matt. 13:47-48)

7. Lord Jesus and my Savior, the one with the key to the bottomless pit. Today, by your Blood, lockup every bottomless pit in my life, my family's life and my descendants' lives, in Jesus' Name. (Rev. 9:1)

8. Jesus Christ, the Faithful Witness, the Firstborn from the dead, and Ruler over kings of the earth; my Father, wash me completely with Your Blood, in Jesus' Name. (Rev.1:5)

9. Lord God, I will give birth to nine Spiritual gifts in me. I give birth to: the word of wisdom, the word of knowledge, faith, healing, miracles, prophecy, discerning of spirits, tongues, and the interpretation of tongues, for the expansion of the Kingdom of God in my life, in Jesus' Name. (1 Corinth. 12:1-11)

10. Almighty God of heaven, inscribe the gifts of faith and obedience into my heart, in the mighty Name of Jesus. (1 Corinth. 12:1-11)

11. Lord, pour Your anointing on me to: exalt every valley, level every mountain, straighten crooked roads, smooth the rough places and let the glory of the LORD be revealed. All flesh will see it together and praise God, in Jesus' Name. (Isa. 40:3-5)

12. Oh Whirlwind of God, arise by fire and denounce every curse working against me. Bring all my blessings to me now, in Jesus' Name. (Rev. 21:10)

13. Father, forgive all my sins and have divine mercy overshadow me, in all areas of my life, in Jesus' Name. (Luke 15:18-19, 18:13)

14. Lord Jesus, send Your grain, new wine and oil to my household and my descendants. I will be satisfied and fruitful, in the mighty Name of Jesus. (Joel 2:19)

15. My Lord Jesus, remove unrighteousness from my household. Let Your eyes be upon me and Your ears open to my prayers, each day of my life, in Jesus' Name. (1 Peter 3:12)

16. Father, let Your Kingdom overshadow me to preach the gospel to all nations, in the Name of Jesus. (Luke 4:18:19)

17. Father, let Your Kingdom come upon my eyes to see the invisible and my ears to hear the inaudible (voice of God). Bless my hands and have my feet level all mountains and hills, in the mighty Name of Jesus. (Isa. 6:9-10)

18. Holy Spirit, manifest Yourself abundantly through me, every day and night of my life, in the mighty Name of Jesus. (John 16:13-14)

19. Lord, send out Holy Ghost and fire to melt the gates of every prison-bound, trap set ahead of me, by the enemy of the gospel, in the Name of Jesus. (Acts 12:6-8)

DAY 20

"Rejoice always, pray without ceasing, in everything give thanks' for this is the will of God in Christ Jesus for you."

1 Thessalonians 5:16-18

Names of Our Lord Jesus Christ:

➢ **Lawgiver:** For the LORD is our judge, the LORD is our lawgiver, the LORD is our king; He will save us. (Isaiah 33:22)

➢ **Lamb:** And all that dwell upon the earth shall worship him, whose names are not written in the book of life of the Lamb slain from the foundation of the world. (Revelation 13:8)

➢ **Lamb of God:** The next day John seeth Jesus coming unto him, and saith, Behold the Lamb of God, which taketh away the sin of the world. (John 1:29)

Declarations and Confessions:

• I receive the key of the house of David, to open the door of prophetic operations.

• I receive the key of the house of David, to open the door of prophetic preaching.

• I receive the key of the house of David, to open the door of prophetic projects.

➢ I receive the key of the house of David, to lockup the door of condemnation.

➢ I receive the key of the house of David, to lockup the door of guilt.

> ➤ I receive the key of the house of David, to lockup the door of shame.

∞ I am justified. (1 Corinthians 6:11)

∞ I am redeemed. (Galatians 3:13)

❖ **Light of God,** insulate me, incubate me and consecrate me.

❖ **Fire of God,** insulate me, incubate me and consecrate me.

❖ **Blood of Jesus,** insulate me, incubate me and consecrate me.

❖ **Holy Ghost Power,** insulate me, incubate me and consecrate me.

(Scriptures: Gen. 1:3; 1:14, Dan. 3:19-25, 1 Pet. 1:2, Act. 1:8; 2:1-4)

Song of Praises:

Praises, Worship and Thanksgiving (Submit yourself to the Lord)

Prayers:

1. Jehovah GOD, do not forget Your Covenant upon my life. Let Your breath of life enter me today. I will stand uprightly and minister Your Word powerfully, in Jesus' Name. (Rev. 11:11)

2. My God, I will obey You forever. Remove from my heart, body, flesh and soul, the spirit of disobedience that will transgress against Your Covenant, in the Name of Jesus. (2 Kings 17:35)

3. The Almighty God, no one comes to Jesus, except You draw them. My Father, I ask You to draw all men to me, in order to disciple and teach them the truth and power in Your Word, in Jesus' Name. (Matt 28:19-20)

4. Lord Jesus, from today onward, I decree all food that I eat and water that I drink, will receive the Blood of Jesus, in the Name of Jesus. (Luke 22:19-20)

5. My Master Lord Jesus, clothe me with Your garments of praise and worship, in Jesus' Name. (Rev. 3:4-5)

6. King of kings, the Kingdom of God is like a king who wanted to settle an account with his servants. My King, remove from me the spirit of un-forgiveness and replace it with the Kingdom principles of adoration, compassion and forgiveness, in the mighty Name of Jesus. (Matt. 18:23-35)

7. Lord Jesus, You are the Savior of my life. I pray by the power in Your Blood to lockup into the bottomless pit, every: dragon, serpent of old, deceitful god and idol, in the mighty name of Jesus. (Rev. 20:1)

8. Lord Jesus, every spiritual animal and evil spirit in my life, receive the Blood of Jesus today, in the mighty Name of Jesus. (Rev. 17:2-8)

9. Lord Jesus, I know You cried at the ninth hour, on the cross for me. Let Your cry, put an end to all my tears and replace them all with joy unspeakable, in Jesus' Name. (Matt 27:46, Rev. 7:17)

10. Lord God, how manifold are Your works, in wisdom You have made them all! In Your power, let these seven mysteries (earth, moon, sun, stars, wind, water, root/herbs) of this world obey and assist me, in every area of my life, in Jesus' Name. (Ps.104:1-end; 104:24, Josh.10:12-13)

11. King of kings and Lord of lords, have every fetish power in my life, catch fire now. LORD of my life, destroy the spirit of "almost there", working against the accomplishment of my goals, in Jesus' Name. (Jer. 5:26)

12. By the Blood of the Lamb, every trap and snare set against me, I send those traps back by fire, to its evil sender, in Jesus' Name. (Jeri. 5:26)

13. Lord Jesus, let Your fountain of living water gush out of me to increase the Kingdom of God and spread Your marvelous Name throughout the earth, in Jesus' Name. (John 4:15)

14. My Lord, as you have done in the parable of the two debtors, You cancelled their debts. Almighty Lord, cancel all debts against me today, in the mighty Name of Jesus. (Luke 7:40-44)

15. Holy Spirit, speak and sing through me, for the work of the ministry for Christ Jesus, in the mighty Name of Jesus. (1 Corinth. 14:15, Eph. 5:19)

16. Holy Spirit, refresh the language of heaven into my mouth, each day of my life, in the mighty Name of Jesus. (1 Corinth. 14:15, Eph. 5:19)

17. Father and my LORD, endow me with Your anointing power against any cost of discipleship, in the mighty Name of Jesus. (Luke 14:28-33)

18. Holy Spirit, refresh and renew me from physical and spiritual burnout, in the mighty Name of Jesus. (Rom. 8:27, Isa 28:12)

19. Holy Ghost, strengthen me continuously with a dose of Your spiritual zeal, in the mighty Name of Jesus. (Acts 18:25)

20. Holy Spirit, release to my hand today, the key to operating with an excellent spirit like Daniel, in the mighty Name of Jesus. (Dan. 5:12; 6:3)

21. Holy Spirit, give me deeper insight into the things of God. My Lord, speak Your heavenly language through me, in the mighty Name of Jesus. (1 Corinth. 12:10, Jude 1:20)

DAY 21

"Therefore, I exhort first of all that supplications, prayers, intercessions, and giving thanks be made for all men, for kings and all who are in authority, that we may lead a quite and peaceable life in all godliness and reverence. For this is good and acceptable in the sight of God our Savior who desires all men to be saved and to come to the knowledge of the truth."

1Timothy 2:1-3

Names of Our Lord Jesus Christ:

➤ **Leader and Commander:** Behold, I have given him for a witness to the people, a leader and commander to the people. (Isaiah 55:4)

➤ **The Life:** Jesus saith unto him, I am the way, the truth, and the life, no man cometh unto the Father, but by me. (John 14:6)

➤ **Light of the World:** Then spake Jesus again unto them, saying, I am the light of the world, he that followeth me shall not walk in darkness, but shall have the light of life. (John 8:12)

Declarations and Confessions:

• I receive the key of the house of David, to open the door of prophetic discernment.

• I receive the key of the house of David, to open the door of the prophetic realm.

• I receive the key of the house of David, to open the door of prophetic authority.

➤ I receive the key of the house of David, to lockup the door of a perverse heart.

➤ I receive the key of the house of David, to lockup the door of filthy dreams.

> ➤ I receive the key of the house of David, to lockup the door of an unclean spirit.

∞ I am forgiven. (Psalms 32:1)

∞ I am washed. (Psalms 51:7)

❖ **Light of God,** insulate me, incubate me and consecrate me.

❖ **Fire of God,** insulate me, incubate me and consecrate me.

❖ **Blood of Jesus,** insulate me, incubate me and consecrate me.

❖ **Holy Ghost Power,** insulate me, incubate me and consecrate me.
(Scriptures: Gen. 1:3; 1:14, Dan. 3:19-25, 1 Pet. 1:2, Act. 1:8; 2:1-4)

Song of Praises:

Praises, Worship and Thanksgiving (Submit yourself to the Lord)

Prayers:

1. Almighty God, Queen Esther found favor with King Ahasuerus. My Lord, let me find favor with all men and presidents of all nations, in Jesus' Name. (Esther 5:8)

2. LORD God of Israel, let the Ark of the Covenant remain permanently in my household and my descendants' household, in the Name of the Lord Jesus Christ. (Num. 10:33; 14:44)

3. The Mighty One of Israel, let Your anointing power fall upon me that will marvel the multitudes. As a result, they will glorify God who is the Most High and also the center of my life, in the Name of Jesus. (Matt. 9:8)

4. Almighty God in heaven, through the Blood of Jesus, I loose and separate myself from every chain of wickedness attached to my: health, children, family, ministry, and finances, in Jesus' Name. (John 11:23-44)

5. Lord Jesus and my Master, clothe me with the garments of humility and obedience, to run this race to the end, in Jesus' Name. (Rev. 5:12; 7:12)

6. Jehovah God, the Kingdom of Heaven is like the landowner who went out early in the morning to hire laborers for his vineyard. My Father, remove the spirit of weariness or tiredness, from working in Your vine-

yard. Today, shower me with the spirit of completion and fulfillment in Your Kingdom. Make me Your faithful chosen laborer, in Jesus' Name. (Matt. 20:1-16)

7. My Father, Son of David and Beholder of the key to the house of David, release to my hand today, the key of: authority, counsel, prosperity, power, wealth, understanding, knowledge, wisdom and revelation of You, in the mighty Name of Jesus. (Isa. 22:22; Matt. 16:19, Rev. 3:7)

8. Lord Jesus Christ and the Mighty One of Israel, baptize me with the Holy Ghost and fire, in the mighty Name of Jesus. (Matt. 3:11)

9. Lord Jesus Christ, with Your precious Blood, I separate from me the four powers of darkness: bottomless pit, ungodly (irreverent), lasciviousness and lightning, mentioned nine times in the Holy Bible, in Jesus' Name. (Rev. 9:1; 20:1-3)

10. LORD God, how manifold are Your works, in wisdom You have made them all. Thank You Lord for the earth and land that obeys and assists me in bringing forth its goodness to me, in Jesus' Name. (Deut. 28:1-3)

11. Almighty God, I decree by Holy Ghost and fire, that I recover every lost blessing from my ancestors today, in Jesus' Name. (Deut. 28:1-14)

12. LORD of Hosts, demonstrate Your power through me to show nations, how big my GOD is to mankind, in Jesus in Name. (2 Kings 1:7-12)

13. Lord Jesus Christ, as You did to the disciples on the day of Pentecost, let the Holy Ghost and fire sit on me, my tongue and every area of my life. Have me heal the crippled to walk, the blind to see, the deaf to hear and the dumb to speak, in the mighty Name of Jesus. (Acts 3: 6-9)

14. Lord God, give no place to the devil, in any area of my life, in the mighty Name of Jesus. (Mark 5:5-19; Matt. 26:47-53)

15. Father, let all my prayers be wrapped in Your Word, so that angels may harken to the Word of God in my life, in the mighty Name of Jesus. (Ps. 103:19-20; Deut. 28:1-14)

16. My Father, let your Holy Spirit overshadow me in prayer, according to Your will in my life, in the mighty Name of Jesus. (Heb. 1:6-14)

17. Father, my prayers will be wrapped in Your Word and angels will harken to the Word of God coming from my mouth. Your angels shall minister salvation to me, in the mighty Name of Jesus. (Heb. 1:6-14, Ps. 103:19-20)

18. Almighty Father, my prayers will be wrapped in Your Word and angels will harken to the Word of God pouring from my mouth, soul and spirit. Your angels shall minister strength to me, in the mighty Name of Jesus. (Heb. 1:6-14)

19. Almighty Father, my prayers will be wrapped in Your Word and angels will harken to the Word of God pouring from my mouth, body, soul and spirit. They shall act according to the will of God in my life, in Jesus Name. (Heb. 1:6-14, Deut. 28:1-14)

DAY 22

"I desire therefore that the men pray everywhere, lifting up holy hands, without wrath and doubting."

1Timothy 2:8

Names of Our Lord Jesus Christ:

> **Lion of the Tribe of Judah:** And one of the elders saith unto me, Weep not: behold, the Lion of the tribe of Judah, the Root of David, hath prevailed to open the book, and to loose the seven seals thereof. (Revelation 5:5)

> **Lord of All:** The word which God sent unto the children of Israel, preaching peace by Jesus Christ: (He is Lord of all:) (Acts 10:36)

> **Lord of Glory:** Which none of the princes of this world knew: for had they known it, they would not have crucified the Lord of glory. (1 Corinthians 2:8)

Declarations and Confessions:

- I receive the key of the house of David, to open the door of prophetic teaching.
- I receive the key of the house of David, to open the door of prophetic visions.
- I receive the key of the house of David, to open the door of prophetic warfare.

> I receive the key of the house of David, to lockup the door of occult sex.

> I receive the key of the house of David, to lockup the door of lust.

> ➤ I receive the key of the house of David, to lockup the door of promiscuity.

∞ I am reconciled. (Romans 5:10)

∞ I am given a new heart. (Ezekiel 36:26)

❖ **Light of God,** insulate me, incubate me and consecrate me.

❖ **Fire of God,** insulate me, incubate me and consecrate me.

❖ **Blood of Jesus,** insulate me, incubate me and consecrate me.

❖ **Holy Ghost Power,** insulate me, incubate me and consecrate me.

(Scriptures: Gen. 1:3; 1:14, Dan. 3:19-25, 1 Pet. 1:2, Act. 1:8; 2:1-4)

Song of Praises:

Praises, Worship and Thanksgiving (Submit yourself to the Lord)

Prayers:

1. Zion of Israel, Job lost all and recovered all that he lost. Grant me Your mercy and grace to recover all stolen blessings, lost blessings and the lost blessings of my ancestors. Restore them all today, in Jesus' Name. (Job 42:10)

2. LORD God, let Your kingdom come into my life as you did to David's kingdom over Israel forever, by Your Covenant of Salt. LORD, I receive dominion over all things on earth, by Your Covenant of Salt, in Jesus' Name. (2 Chron. 13:5)

3. Lord Jesus, I receive the anointing power to: heal the sick, the blind to see, the deaf to hear, the dumb to speak, the lame to walk and the oppressed to be set free, in the mighty Name of Jesus. (Acts 3:6-10)

4. Lord Jesus, heal me from all sin and I will have victory over: bitterness, bondages, demons, disease, greed, evil spirits, pride, drunkenness, gossip, greed, envy and disobedience, in the Name of Jesus. (Rev. 9:1; 20:1-3)

5. The Creator of heaven and earth, clothe me with the garment of holiness, in Jesus' Name. (Rev. 3:5, Deut. 24:17)

6. Lord of lords, the Kingdom of heaven is like a certain king who arranged a marriage for his son. My Father, do not cast me into outer darkness, but choose me among the many you have called, in Jesus' Name. (Matt. 22:1-14)

7. Almighty God, Your mercy and grace abide in Your Word. Let Your Light shine upon my heart, from Your spoken parables. Grant me understanding for the expansion of Your Kingdom, in Jesus' Name. (1 Tim. 1:2, Isa. 11:2-3)

8. My Lord Jesus Christ, today I receive the key of understanding Your Scriptures from Genesis through Revelation. I will share Your Word with all brethren and nations, in Jesus' Name. (Matt. 16:18-19, Rev. 7:12)

9. Lord Jesus, as You did on the day of Pentecost, let sound come from heaven like a rushing mighty wind. Fill my house and sit on me. Fill me Holy Spirit to make utterances like liquid fire, in Jesus' Name. (Acts 2:2-3)

10. Almighty GOD, as nine marked the end of single digit numbers, let all my: trouble, sorrow, calamity, disappointment, tragedy, sickness, shame, poverty, lack and unfruitfulness, since the day of my birth, end today by fire, in Jesus' Name. (Rev. 9:1; 20:1-3)

11. El Shaddai, the Almighty, how manifold are Your works, in wisdom You have made them all. Mystery of moon and Sun, obey and assist me to bring forth the goodness of the land to me, in Jesus' Name. (Deut. 28:1-14)

12. LORD of Hosts, reveal yourself to me and use me like You have used all the ancient men who feared You, in the Name of Jesus. (Zech. 8:23)

13. Lord Jesus Christ, as You did to Ananias and Sapphira, on behalf of Peter; make me a carrier of the Holy Ghost to destroy the enemy of the church and the enemy of my soul, in Jesus' Name. (Acts 5: 1-10)

14. Almighty God, I stand boldly on the ground of the Blood of Jesus. I proclaim victory over sin, satan, his agents and the world, in the Name of Jesus Christ. (Rev. 3:5)

15. Almighty God, through the precious Blood of Jesus, I have been redeemed out of the hands of the devil, in Jesus' Name. (2 Sam. 18:8; Rev 3:5)

16. LORD of Hosts, through the Blood of Jesus; I am justified, sanctified and made holy with God's holiness, in the mighty Name of Jesus. (Heb. 10:19)

17. Almighty God of Israel, I close every door of strange legs walking against my life and destiny, in the mighty Name of Jesus. (Jer. 5:26)

18. Ancients of days, I close and bind every strange leg operating in my: destiny, ministry, business, marriage, prosperity and wealth now, in the mighty Name of Jesus. (Jer. 5:26)

19. Almighty God, I pray O' LORD, that You will continue to use all Christian television networks across the globe, to spread Good News of Lord Jesus Christ, in the mighty name of Jesus. (Matt. 27:18-20)

DAY 23

"Is anyone among you suffering? Let him pray. Is anyone cheerful? Let him sing psalms."

James 5:13

Names of Our Lord Jesus Christ:

➤ **Lord of lords:** Which in his times he shall show, who is the blessed and only Potentate, the King of kings, and Lord of lords. (1 Timothy 6:15)

➤ **Lord of Our Righteousness:** In his days Judah shall be saved, and Israel shall dwell safely; and this is his name whereby he shall be called, THE LORD OUR RIGHTEOUSNESS. (Jeremiah 23:6)

➤ **Man of Sorrows:** He is despised and rejected of men; a man of sorrows, and acquainted with grief: and we hid as it were our faces from him; he was despised, and we esteemed him not. *(Isaiah 53:3)*

➤ **Mediator:** For there is one God, and one mediator between God and men, the man Christ Jesus. (1 Timothy 2:5)

Declarations and Confessions:

• I receive the key of the house of David, to open the door of prophetic watch-care.

• I receive the key of the house of David, to open the door of prophetic wisdom.

• I receive the key of the house of David, to open the door of prophetic economy.

➢ I receive the key of the house of David, to lock up the door of lasciviousness.

➢ I receive the key of the house of David, to lock up the door of prostitution.

➢ I receive the key of the house of David, to lock up the door of sexual perversion.

∞ I am given the Holy Spirit. (1 Corinthians 2:12)

∞ I am given the mind of Christ. (1 Corinthians 2:16)

❖ **Light of God,** insulate me, incubate me and consecrate me.

❖ **Fire of God,** insulate me, incubate me and consecrate me.

❖ **Blood of Jesus,** insulate me, incubate me and consecrate me.

❖ **Holy Ghost Power,** insulate me, incubate me and consecrate me.

(Scriptures: Gen. 1:3; 1:14, Dan. 3:19-25, 1 Pet. 1:2, Act. 1:8; 2:1-4)

Song of Praises:

Praises, Worship and Thanksgiving (Submit yourself to the Lord)

Prayers:

1. LORD of Hosts, as You did for David; forgive all my iniquities, restore to me the joy of Your salvation and uphold me by Your generous Spirit, in Jesus' Name. (Ps. 51:12).

2. Mighty God of Israel by Your covenant of earth, water, sun, star, moon, wind, roots and herbs; bring forth the goodness of the land to me today, in the mighty Name of Jesus. (Deut. 28:1-4)

3. Almighty God of Heaven, let the Holy Ghost come upon me and the power of the Highest overshadow me. LORD, let the great work of God begin and expand significantly in my life, in Jesus' Name. (Luke 1:35)

4. Almighty Father, according to the parable of the two sons; Lord Jesus, remove completely the spirit of disobedience and unbelief in my life and my family's life, in Jesus' Name. (Matt. 21:28-30)

5. Lord Jesus Christ, heal me. Today, I receive Your miracle healing power from all sin: excessiveness, gluttony, covetousness, idolatry, immorality, infirmity, jealousy, laziness, poverty, impurity and impatience, in the Name of Jesus. (Rev. 9:1, 20:1-3)

6. Lord Jesus, every one of my enemies running after my garments, like they did to Joseph to truncate his

destiny; let my enemies receive total shame, disgrace and the fire of God, in the Name of Jesus. (Rev. 3:5)

7. Almighty Father, according to the parable of the two sons; Lord Jesus, remove the spirit of disobedience and unbelief in my life and replace it with the spirit of obedience and belief. Lord, do not cast me out, but choose me among the many you have called, in Jesus' Name. (Matt. 21:28-30)

8. Jesus of Nazareth and Son of David, I receive the keys to: administration, finance, military, warfare and foreign affairs of the land, as your true ambassador on earth, in Jesus' Name. (Matt. 16:19)

9. The ancient of Days, today and forever; I receive Holy Ghost power to witness about the Lord Jesus in Jerusalem, Judea, Samaria and to the ends of earth, in the mighty Name of Jesus. (Act. 1:8)

10. Almighty God, let every pending issue in my life receive a positive conclusion this month, in Jesus' Name. (James 2:13)

11. LORD God, how manifold are Your works, in wisdom You have made them all. Mystery of stars and wind, obey and assist me to bring forth the goodness of the land in my life, in Jesus Name. (Ps. 104: 25; Deut. 28:1-14)

12. Lord GOD, concerning my destiny, let every power of darkness go to the bottomless pit today, in the mighty Name of Jesus. (Rev. 20:1-3)

13. Lord Jesus, remove physical and spiritual blindness from my eyes and every negative thing attached to my name. Make me Your true ambassador here on earth, in Jesus' Name. (Acts 9:17-18)

14. Ancient of days, I confess today, my body is the temple of the Holy Spirit. I am redeemed, cleansed and sanctified by the Blood of the Lamb. satan you and your constituencies have no place in me and have no power over me or my family, in the mighty Name of Jesus Christ. (Isa 45:23)

15. Holy Spirit, dominate my life completely, to pray according to the will and desire of God from His throne, in Jesus' Name. (Ps. 103:19-20)

16. Holy Spirit, every prayer proceeding from my mouth, will bring the blessings of God to me, in Jesus' Name. (Ps. 34:7; 91:11, Dan. 6:22, Matt. 2:13,19; 4:11; Luke 22:43, Acts 5:19)

17. LORD of Hosts, let angels minister salvation, physical safety and well being to me, in the mighty Name of Jesus. (Ps. 34:7; 91:11, Dan. 6.:22, Matt. 2:13,19; 4:11, Luke 22:43, Acts 5:19)

18. Almighty God of heaven, You have set apart and employed the angel Prince Michael and Gabriel for services to favor Daniel, Mary, Joseph, Zacharias and Elizabeth. Lord Jesus harken angels to the Word of God coming from my mouth, favoring me in all areas of my life, in Jesus' Name. (Dan. 8:16,19, 21; Luke 1:19, 26; Dan. 10:13, 21)

19. Almighty God, the Word of God coming from my mouth through prayer, will bring abundant blessings to me and my descendants, in the mighty Name of Jesus' Name. (Dan. 8:16,19:21; Luke 1:19, 26; Dan. 10:13, 21)

DAY 24

"Is anyone among you sick? Let him call for the elders of the church, and let them pray over him, anointing him with oil in the name of the Lord,"

James 5:14

Names of Our Lord Jesus Christ:

- ➤ **Messenger of the Covenant:** Behold, I will send my messenger, and he shall prepare the way before me: and the Lord, whom ye seek, shall suddenly come to his temple, even the messenger of the covenant, whom ye delight in: behold, he shall come, saith the LORD of hosts. (Malachi 3:1)

- ➤ **Messiah:** Know therefore and understand, that from the going forth of the commandment to restore and to build Jerusalem unto the Messiah the Prince shall be seven weeks, and threescore and two weeks: the street shall be built again, and the wall, even in troublous times. (Daniel 9:25)

- ➤ **Mighty God:** For unto us a child is born, unto us a son is given: and the government shall be upon his shoulders: and his name shall be called Wonderful, Counselor, The mighty God, The everlasting Father, The Prince of Peace. (Isaiah 9:6)

- ➤ **Mighty One:** Thou shall also suck the milk of the Gentiles, and shall suck the breast of kings: and thou shall know that I the LORD am thy Savior and thy Redeemer, the mighty One of Jacob. (Isaiah 60:16)

Declarations and Confessions:

- I receive the key of the house of David, to open the door of the prophetic mantle.
- I receive the key of the house of David, to open the door to prophetic dreams.
- I receive the key of the house of David, to open the door of prophetic visions.

- ➤ I receive the key of the house of David, to lockup the door of the spirit of compromise.
- ➤ I receive the key of the house of David, to lockup the door of mental illness.
- ➤ I receive the key of the house of David, to lockup the door of unreasonable behavior.

- ∞ I am given strength from God. (Psalms 29:11)
- ∞ I am given the mercy of God. (Ezekiel 33:19)

- ❖ **Light of God,** insulate me, incubate me and consecrate me.
- ❖ **Fire of God,** insulate me, incubate me and consecrate me.
- ❖ **Blood of Jesus,** insulate me, incubate me and consecrate me.

❖ **Holy Ghost Power,** insulate me, incubate me and con-secrate me.

(Scriptures: Gen. 1:3; 1:14, Dan. 3:19-25, 1 Pet. 1:2, Act. 1:8; 2:1-4)

Song of Praises:

Praises, Worship and Thanksgiving (Submit yourself to the Lord)

Prayers:

1. My Lord God, do not incline my heart to anything evil in the world nor join wicked men who walk and work in iniquity. Father, do not allow me to eat from their delicacies, in Jesus' Name. (Ps. 141:4)

2. LORD, give me the strength to enter Your sanctuary with Your covenant inscribed upon my heart. May I seek You, Lord, with all my heart and with all my soul, in the mighty Name of Jesus. (2 Chron. 15:12)

3. Thou great power of God, over shadow me today and nullify all sources of sin in my life, through the precious Blood of Jesus Christ, in the mighty Name of Jesus. (Acts 5: 4)

4. Lord Jesus, heal my body, soul and spirit completely, from any illness or disease of the land, in Jesus' Name. (Exod. 15:26)

5. Almighty God, every one of my garments that the enemy has stolen from me, from birth until now, let them catch the fire of God, in Jesus' Name. (Rev. 3:5)

6. Lord, the Bridegroom, according to the parable of the ten virgins with lamps, I refuse all foolishness. Lord Jesus, please keep my lamp burning like the five wise virgins, in the Name of Jesus. (Matt. 25:1-13)

7. Mighty One and Powerful of Israel, release into my hands the key to prayer and fasting, in Jesus' Name. (Matt. 16:19; 17:20-21)

8. LORD of Hosts, I pray according to Your will, that I hear to understand and see to perceive. Father, turn my stony heart to flesh, in Jesus Name. (Isa. 6:9-10)

9. God that cannot be disgraced, let the fire of God fall and consume my enemies and their helpers. Turn their gods and idols to ashes, in the mighty Name of Jesus. (1 Kings 18:25-38, 2 Kings 1:9-15, Ezek. 12:14-16)

10. Holy Ghost and fire, purge out by fire and bury permanently, all evil trees planted in my life, in Jesus' Name. (Mark 11:12-24)

11. Jesus Christ, the Lamb of God, by the power in the Blood of Jesus, I blind every evil eye monitoring my destiny, in the mighty of Name of Jesus. (Acts 13:8-11, Zech. 14:12)

12. Almighty God of Heaven, I cancel every situation from the first Edenic Covenant in my life and replace it completely with the redemptive New Covenant, of the Lord Jesus Christ, in His Name. (Gen. 2:16)

13. Almighty God of Heaven, I cancel every condition of the second Adamic Covenant and receive the redemptive New Covenant, of the Lord Jesus Christ, in the

mighty Name of Jesus. (Gen. 3:15, John 12:31, Gal. 4:4)

14. Almighty God of Heaven, I move from the situation of the third Noahic Covenant and replace it with the promise of the redemptive New Covenant of Jesus Christ, in the mighty Name of Jesus. (Gen. 9:16, Col. 2:9)

15. Almighty God of Heaven, I receive the forth Abrahamic Covenant with additions to the redemptive New Covenant of Jesus Christ, in the mighty Name of Jesus. (Gen. 12:2; 22:18, Gal. 3:16, Phil. 2:8)

16. Almighty God of Heaven, I reject completely the fifth Mosaic Covenant and replace it with the redemptive New Covenant of Jesus Christ, in the mighty Name of Jesus. (Exod. 19:5, Rom. 3:23, 5:12, Gal. 3:10-13)

17. Almighty God of Heaven, remove from me the sixth Palestinian Covenant and replace it completely with the redemptive New Covenant of the Lord Jesus Christ, in the mighty Name of Jesus. (Deut. 30:3, 28:1-30: 9)

18. Almighty God of Heaven, establish the perpetuity of the seventh Davidic Covenant with the redemptive New Covenant of Jesus Christ in my life, in the mighty Name of Jesus. (2 Sam. 7:16, Matt. 1:1, Luke 1:31-33, 1 Corinth. 15:24)

19. Almighty God of Heaven, I receive the unconditional eighth New Covenant of the Lord Jesus Christ, in the mighty Name of Jesus. (Matt. 26:28, 1 Corinth. 11:25, Heb. 8:8, Gal. 3:13-19)

DAY 25

"And the prayer of faith will save the sick, and the Lord will raise him up. And if he has committed sins, he will be forgiven."

James 5:15

Names of Our Lord Jesus Christ:

- ➢ **Morning Star:** I Jesus have sent mine angel to testify unto you these things in the churches. I am the root and the offspring of David, and the bright and morning star. (Revelation 22:16)

- ➢ **Nazarene:** And he came and dwelt in a city called Nazareth: that it might be fulfilled which was spoken by the prophets, He shall be called a Nazarene. (Matthew 2:23)

- ➢ **Only Begotten Son:** No man hath seen God at any time; the only begotten Son, which is in the bosom of the Father, he hath declared him. (John 1:18)

- ➢ **Our Passover:** Purge out therefore the old leaven, that ye may be a new lump, as ye are unleavened. For even Christ Our Passover is sacrificed for us: (1 Corinthians 5:7)

Declarations and Confessions:

- • I receive the key of the house of David, to open the door of discipleship.
- • I receive the key of the house of David, to open the door of the seven Spirits of God.
- • I receive the key of the house of David, to open the door of Abrahamic Covenant blessings

> ➤ I receive the key of the house of David, to lockup the door of impotence.
> ➤ I receive the key of the house of David, to lockup the door of satanic traps.
> ➤ I receive the key of the house of David, to lockup the door of evil and idolatrous inheritances.

∞ I am given the grace of God. (James 4:6)

∞ I am given complete access to God. (Ephesians 3:12)

❖ **Light of God,** insulate me, incubate me and consecrate me.

❖ **Fire of God,** insulate me, incubate me and consecrate me.

❖ **Blood of Jesus,** insulate me, incubate me and consecrate me.

❖ **Holy Ghost Power,** insulate me, incubate me and consecrate me.

(Scriptures: Gen. 1:3; 1:14, Dan. 3:19-25, 1 Pet. 1:2, Act. 1:8; 2:1-4)

Song of Praises:

Praises, Worship and Thanksgiving (Submit yourself to the Lord)

Prayers:

1. Lord Jesus, separate sin (spirit of gathering and collecting) from me. Grant me Your wisdom, knowledge and joy as a man who is good in your sight, in Jesus' Name. (Eccl. 2:26)

2. LORD, thou Covenant of Salt as it is for the House of David, let it begin to work for me, my family and my descendants, in the mighty Name of Jesus. (Num. 18:19)

3. Thou great Power of God, anointed Jesus of Nazareth with the Holy Ghost and with power: He went about doing good, and healing those oppressed of the devil. Anoint me with Your power, in Jesus' mighty Name. (Acts 10:38)

4. My Lord, heal me today. Let every disease or sickness planted in my life by the power of darkness, dry up and wither from the root now, like the fig tree, in Jesus' Name. (Mark 11:12-24)

5. Almighty God, clothe me with the garments of a warrior in Your kingdom to face the enemy of the church and my life, in the Name of Jesus. (Acts 5:1-11; 16: 23-29)

6. Lord and my Master, according to the parable of the talents; Lord Jesus, remove the spirit of wickedness

and laziness from me and replace it with productive talent, in Jesus' Name. (Matt. 25:14-30)

7. Jehovah GOD, the Giver of all gifts, endow me with Your precious key to resolve every problem presented to me, for the expansion of Your Kingdom, in the mighty Name of Jesus. (Matt. 16:19)

8. LORD that answers by fire, today and every day of my life, answer all my prayers by fire, in the mighty Name of Jesus. (1 Kings 18:24)

9. Holy Ghost, I reject and terminate all evil dreams today. I will give birth to great dreams, visions and revelations, to expand the Kingdom of God, in Jesus' Name. (Dan. 2:19-23)

10. Almighty God of Heaven, inscribe in my heart the gift of fasting and prayer: to loose the bonds of wicked-ness, to undo heavy burdens, to let the oppressed go free and break every yoke in all the brethren, in Jesus' Name. (Matt. 17:21, Isa. 58:6)

11. God of Heaven, I decree all evil animals sent by my household enemies to attack me, now receive the Lion of Judah and be torn into pieces, in the mighty Name of Jesus. (Dan. 7:1-8)

12. Father, as You healed Aeneas from paralysis and raised Dorcas from dead, I decree everything that has been paralyzed and dead in my life: finances, health,

career and ministry; receive strength and full resurrection power, in the mighty Name of Jesus. (Acts 9:33-41; 20:9-10)

13. Lord God, how manifold are Your works, in wisdom You have made them all. Mystery of water, roots and herbs; obey and assist me to bring forth the goodness of the land, in Jesus' Name. (Deut. 28:1-14; Ps. 104:24)

14. Lord Jesus, all traps set by the power of darkness to catch me; I command those traps to search for and catch all my enemies, in the mighty Name of Jesus. (Jer. 5:26)

15. Lord Jesus, worthy is the Lamb who was slain. Today I receive power, riches and wisdom to work in Your vineyard, in the mighty Name of Jesus. (Rev. 5:12a)

16. Lord Jesus, worthy is the Lamb who was slain. Today I receive strength and honor to work in your vineyard, in the mighty Name of Jesus. (Rev. 5:12b)

17. Lord Jesus, worthy is the Lamb who was slain. Today I receive glory and blessing to work in your vineyard, in the mighty Name of Jesus. (Rev. 5:12b)

18. Jehovah Lord, remove and wipe off with the Blood of Jesus, every reproach in my life, in the Name of Jesus. (Matt. 26:6)

19. Mighty God, remove all hindrances (sin, un-forgiveness, disobedience, unbelief, selfishness, pride, dishonoring my spouse) to an effective prayer from me, in Jesus' Name. (Ps. 66:18, Matt. 6:14-15, Mark 11:25-26, Prov. 28:9, James 1:6-7, James 4:3, Luke 18:9-14, 1Pet. 3:7, 1 Corinth. 7:1-6)

DAY 26

"Confess your trespasses to one another, and pray for one another, that you may be healed. The effective, fervent prayer of a righteous man avails much."

James 5:16

Names of Our Lord Jesus Christ:

> **Prince of Life:** And killed the Prince of life, whom God hath raised from the dead; whereof we are witnesses. (Acts 3:15)

> **Prince of Kings:** And from Jesus Christ, who is the faithful witness, and the first begotten of the dead, and the prince of the kings of the earth. Unto him that loved us, and washed us from our sins in his own blood. (Revelation 1:5)

> **Prince of Peace:** For unto us a child is born, unto us a son is given: and the government shall be upon his shoulder: and his name shall be called Wonderful, Counselor, The mighty God, The everlasting Father, The Prince of Peace. (Isaiah 9:6)

> **Prophet:** And he said unto them, What things? And they said unto him, Concerning Jesus of Nazareth, which was a prophet mighty in deed and word before God and all the people. (Luke 24:19)

Declarations and Confessions:

- I receive the key of the house of David, to open the door of being right with God.
- I receive the key of the house of David, to open the door to freedom in Christ.

- I receive the key of the house of David, to open the door of reading and understanding scriptures.

➢ I receive the key of the house of David, to lockup the door of depression.

➢ I receive the key of the house of David, to lockup the door of barrenness.

➢ I receive the key of the house of David, to lockup the door of premature aging and death.

∞ I am given everything for life and godliness. (2 Peter 1:3)

∞ I am created to do good works. (Ephesians 2:10)

❖ **Light of God,** insulate me, incubate me and consecrate me.

❖ **Fire of God,** insulate me, incubate me and consecrate me.

❖ **Blood of Jesus,** insulate me, incubate me and consecrate me.

❖ **Holy Ghost Power,** insulate me, incubate me and consecrate me.

(Scriptures: Gen. 1:3; 1:14, Dan. 3:19-25, 1 Pet. 1:2, Act. 1:8; 2:1-4)

Song of Praises:

Praises, Worship and Thanksgiving (Submit yourself to the Lord)

Prayers:

1. LORD, according to Your Word, let the Spirit of God rest upon me. The Spirit of wisdom, understanding, counsel, might, knowledge and the fear of the Lord, in Jesus' Name. (Isa. 11: 2)

2. My God, the great, the mighty, and the terrible God who keeps covenant and mercy. Remove all sins of the land from me, my family and their descendants, in Jesus' Name. (Neh. 9:32)

3. LORD God of hope, fill me with all joy and peace in believing that I may abound in hope, through the mighty power of the Holy Ghost, in the mighty Name of Jesus. (Rom. 15:13)

4. Almighty God and my great Physician, renew my flesh, bones and blood with the precious flesh and blood of Jesus Christ, in Jesus' Name. (Esther 5:1-4)

5. Yahweh, cover my garments and shoes with Your anointing that is poisonous to the enemy of my life, in the mighty Name of Jesus. (Isa. 14:29-30)

6. God, the Mighty Shepherd, according to the parable of the judgment of nations as sheep separated from the goats. Lord Jesus, consecrate and perfect me among the faithful sheep found in Your right hand, in the mighty Name of Jesus. (Matt. 25:31-46)

7. Jehovah God and the Giver of all gifts, endow me with Your precious keys to: raise the dead, heal the sick, the dumb to speak, the deaf to hear and the crippled to walk, in the mighty Name of Jesus. (Matt. 16:19, Isa. 22:22)

8. LORD, as You have done for ancient men through fire, let your fire work for me in all areas of my life, in the mighty Name of Jesus. (2 Kings 1:10-15)

9. Lord of lords and King of kings, destroy all evil work planted against me and the church, in Jesus' Name. (Matt. 3:10)

10. Almighty God of all grace, who called me to His eternal glory in Christ Jesus, I have suffered a while. My Savior, perfect me, establish me, strengthen me and settle me, in all areas of my life, in Jesus' Name. (1 Pet. 5:10)

11. Almighty God, I pray all spiritual property of mine that household enemies are sitting on, now receive the fire of the Holy Ghost, in Jesus' Name. (Rev. 2: 20-23)

12. My Creator, whatever the enemy has taken from my body to do evil, I recover all by the fire of the Holy Ghost. I cancel all their activities upon me, my family and their descendants, in the mighty Name of Jesus. (Rev. 2: 20-23)

13. Father, anoint me with Your great power to cure: lameness, blindness, deafness, dumbness, mental illness, unreasonable behavior and demon possession, in the mighty Name of Jesus. (Acts 14:8-10; 16:16-18; 28:7-9)

14. Father of Light, bless me O Lord and grant me mercy to endure and abstain from the temptation of evil. I receive the crown of life which you have promised to those who love You, in the mighty Name of Jesus. (James 1:12)

15. Merciful God of Light, remove from me all filthiness and any overflow of wickedness. I receive meekness from the Word of God implanted in me, in Jesus' Name. (James 1: 21)

16. My Father, I will triumph over all solicitation of evil, test of purpose, test of obedience, test of true religion, test of brotherly love, test of good works and test of faith, in the mighty Name of Jesus. (James.1, 2)

17. My Father, implant in me the desire to do Your work effectively for the expansion of Your kingdom, in the mighty Name of Jesus. (James 2:14-18)

DAY 27

"Beloved, I pray that you may prosper in all things and be in health, just as your soul prospers."

3 John 2

Names of Our Lord Jesus Christ:

➢ **Redeemer:** For I know that my redeemer liveth, and that he shall stand at the latter day upon the earth. (Job 19:25)

➢ **Resurrection and Life:** Jesus said unto her, I am the resurrection, and the life: he that believeth in me, though he were dead, yet shall he live. (John 11:25)

➢ **Rock:** And did all drink the same spiritual drink: for they drank of that spiritual Rock that followed them: and that Rock was Christ. (1 Corinthians 10:4)

➢ **Root of David:** I Jesus have sent mine angel to testify unto you these things in the churches. I am the root and the offspring of David, and the bright and morning star. (Revelation 22:16)

Declarations and Confessions:

• I receive the key of the house of David, to open the door of comfort, in Christ Jesus.

• I receive the key of the house of David, to open the door of wisdom in the LORD.

• I receive the key of the house of David, to open the door to the word of knowledge.

➢ I receive the key of the house of David, to lockup the door of personal disorder.

➤ I receive the key of the house of David, to lockup the door of mental blindness.

➤ I receive the key of the house of David, to lockup the door of using pain killers.

∞ I am an ambassador for Christ. (2 Corinthians 5:20)

∞ I am being conformed to Christ. (Romans 8:29)

❖ **Light of God,** insulate me, incubate me and consecrate me.

❖ **Fire of God,** insulate me, incubate me and consecrate me.

❖ **Blood of Jesus,** insulate me, incubate me and consecrate me.

❖ **Holy Ghost Power,** insulate me, incubate me and consecrate me.

(Scriptures: Gen. 1:3; 1:14, Dan. 3:19-25, 1 Pet. 1:2, Act. 1:8; 2:1-4)

Song of Praises:

Praises, Worship and Thanksgiving (Submit yourself to the Lord)

Prayers:

1. Merciful God of Israel, let Your Spirit breath through me to speak life to every dead bone in the valley to live, stand and build an exceedingly great army for Christ Jesus, in His mighty Name. (Ezek. 37:1-14)

2. My LORD, I seek Your face today. My Father let me: hear through Your ears, see through Your eyes, smell through Your nose, touch with Your hands, speak with Your mouth, feel with Your heart, walk in Your steps and think with Your mind, in the mighty Name of Jesus. (Gen. 2:7, Isa. 6:9-10)

3. Great God of Battle, anoint me with power that parts the red sea, buries all idols and all false gods, in the Name of Jesus. (Exod. 15:1-27, Acts 19:17-20)

4. My Lord Jesus, with Your precious Blood; make my blood, flesh and bones immune from all diseases of the land. Lord, cover me with Your finger, in the Name of Jesus. (Exod. 8:18-19, Isa. 53:4-6)

5. Almighty God, cover me with the garment of fasting and prayer: to loose the bonds of wickedness, undo heavy burdens, set the oppressed to go free and break every yoke, in Jesus' Name. (Isa. 58:6)

6. My Lord and my Master, according to the parable of the good Samaritan; Lord Jesus, circumcise my heart

with Your heavenly sword to reveal the truth in Your Word, in Jesus' Name. (Luke 11:30-36)

7. Almighty God and the Giver of all gifts. Endow me with Your precious keys of truth in all areas of my life. Today, the Word of God in my mouth will bring salvation to all nations, in Jesus Name. (Isa. 22:22, Matt. 16:19)

8. LORD, as you have done for ancient men through light, let Your light work for me in all areas of my life, in the mighty Name of Jesus. (Isa. 60:19)

9. Lord Jesus, in this month of delivery; every good thing I have conceived, may I give birth to them today. Lord, have them flourish and salted with fire, in the Name of Jesus. (Mark 9:49)

10. My Lord Jesus, yield my heart to overflowing with good and my tongue as the pen of a ready writer, in the mighty Name of Jesus. (Ps. 45:1)

11. Father, You equipped Solomon with great wisdom. Lord please grant me wisdom, exceedingly great understanding and a large heart, abundantly, in the mighty Name of Jesus. (1 Kings 4: 29-30)

12. Father and my LORD, I reject by fire any evil testimonies from household enemies, on my life. Today, I command all evil, spiritual soldiers assigned to mon-

itor my life, receive physical and spiritual blindness, in Jesus' Name. (Acts 16: 25-29)

13. Lord Almighty, I receive wisdom from above that is: pure, peaceable, gentle, willing to yield, full of mercy and good fruit, in the mighty Name of Jesus. (James 3:17)

14. Lord, reveal some of the hidden manna that I may eat, both physically and spiritually. Father, I receive by fire, a new name which is written on a white stone, in Jesus' Name. (Rev. 2:26)

15. Lord Jesus, I will hold the tail of the poisonous snake and it will not hurt me. I will walk in the lion's den and it will not attack me. I will have dominion over all things on the earth, above and below, in Jesus' Name. (Gen. 1:26, Acts 28:3-5)

16. Father, remove from me and my midst, all: envy, self-ishness, confusion and every evil thing, in the mighty Name of Jesus. (James 3:16)

17. LORD and my Father, keep my household and their descendants from eating: the bread of sorrow, the bread of adversity and the water of affliction, in the mighty Name of Jesus. (Isa. 30:20; Ps.127:2b)

18. LORD and my Father, keep my household and their descendants from eating: the bread of idleness, the

bread of wickedness and drinking the wine of violence, in the mighty Name of Jesus. (Prov. 4:17; 31:27)

DAY 28

"Husband, likewise, dwell with them with understanding, giving honor to the wife, as to the weaker vessel, and as being heirs together of the grace of life, that your prayers may not be hindered."

1 Peter 3:7

Names of Our Lord Jesus Christ:

- ➤ **Rose of Sharon:** I am the rose of Sharon, and the lily of the valleys. (Song of Songs 2:1)
- ➤ **Savior:** For unto you is born this day in the city of David a Saviour, which is Christ the Lord. (Luke 2:11)
- ➤ **Seed of Woman:** And I will put enmity between thee and the woman, and between thy seed and her seed; it shall bruise thy head, and thou shalt bruise his heel. (Genesis 3:15)
- ➤ **Shepherd and Bishop of Souls:** for ye were as sheep going astray; but are now returned unto the Shepherd and Bishop of your souls. (1 Peter 2:25)

Declarations and Confessions:

- I receive the key of the house of David, to open the door of the Davidic covenant.
- I receive the key of the house of David, to open the door of the New Covenant.
- I receive the key of the house of David, to open the door of the working, miracle power of God.

- ➤ I receive the key of the house of David, to lockup the door of drug abuse.
- ➤ I receive the key of the house of David, to lockup the door of a dull mind.

➢ I receive the key of the house of David, to lockup the door of premature death.

∞ I am complete in Christ. (Colossians 2:10)

∞ I am holy. (1 Thessalonians 4:7)

❖ **Light of God,** insulate me, incubate me and consecrate me.

❖ **Fire of God,** insulate me, incubate me and consecrate me.

❖ **Blood of Jesus,** insulate me, incubate me and consecrate me.

❖ **Holy Ghost Power,** insulate me, incubate me and consecrate me.

(Scriptures: Gen. 1:3; 1:14, Dan. 3:19-25, 1 Pet. 1:2, Act. 1:8; 2:1-4)

Song of Praises:

Praises, Worship and Thanksgiving (Submit yourself to the Lord)

Prayers:

1. Lord Jesus, reveal to me the mysteries of Your Kingdom in all of Your spoken parables, for the expansion of Your Kingdom on earth, in Jesus' Name. (Matt. 13 1-52)

2. My LORD, according to the Covenant of Salt, my household, their descendants and all that concerns me, will be seasoned with fire. Every sacrifice will be seasoned with salt, in Jesus' Name. (Gen. 4:4, Mark 9:49,)

3. Lord Jesus Christ, through mighty signs and wonders and by the power of the Spirit of God in me, let me preach the gospel of Christ to all nations, in Jesus' mighty Name. (Rom. 15:19)

4. King of kings and Lord of lords, every generational illness and inherited disease, let the precious Blood of Jesus remove them from me today, in the mighty Name of Jesus. (Luke 5:31-32)

5. Lord Jesus, let every garment I wear receive Your everlasting light forever, in Jesus' Name. (Isa. 60: 19-20)

6. Lord my Master, according to the parable of the barren fig tree; I cancel every tree of barrenness in my life and replace them with trees of fruitfulness, in Jesus'

Name. (Luke 13-6-9, Mark 11:12-14, 20-23, John 1:48-50, Matt. 24:32-35)

7. Everlasting Father, endow me with Your key to speak to the hearts of: Muslims, Buddhists, Jews, New Age followers, back-sliders, saved and unsaved, in Jesus' Name. (Matt. 16:18-19)

8. LORD, as you have done for all ancient believers through Your Son's Blood, let the Blood of Jesus Christ work for me in all areas of my life, in the mighty Name of Jesus. (Matt. 26:28)

9. LORD and the only One that can speak by fire, let Your fire consume every iniquity in my hands and cleanse me from all my sins. Bring me closer to You each day of my life, in Jesus' Name. (Ps. 144:1)

10. Almighty God of heaven, from today onward, I will feed the poor and heal the sick, in Jesus' Name. (Matt. 5:1-13)

11. Father of Mercies and God of all Comfort; comfort me in all areas of my life and strengthen me to use the comfort which You have endowed me with, to comfort others, in Jesus' Name. (2 Corinth. 1:4)

12. Almighty God, remove from me today, every tree of limitation residing over my destiny and ministry, in the mighty Name of Jesus. (John 1:43-50)

13. Lord GOD, let the precious Blood of Jesus cleanse my body and make me whole from all marks of: wizards, witches, evil and familiar spirits, in the mighty Name of Jesus Christ. (Mark 14:24, Matt. 26:28)

14. Lord Jesus, keep me by the power of Holy Ghost from: all things offered to idols, all things strangled, ritual blood use and from sexual immorality, in the mighty Name of Jesus. (Acts 15:29)

15. Holy Ghost and fire, dwell in me today and bring supernatural health to my physical body, in the mighty Name of Jesus. (Rom. 8:11)

16. Father, let the indwelling Holy Spirit produce the supernatural fear of God in me, my family and their descendants, in the mighty Name of Jesus. (Isa. 11:2)

17. Father, let the indwelling Holy Spirit produce supernatural power and counsel in me, my family and their descendants, in the mighty Name of Jesus. (Isa. 11:2)

18. Father, let the indwelling Holy Spirit produce supernatural wisdom and understanding in me, my family and their descendants, in the mighty Name of Jesus. (Isa. 11:2)

19. Father, let the indwelling Holy Spirit produce supernatural knowledge in me, my family and their descendants, in the mighty Name of Jesus. (Isa. 11:2)

20. Holy Spirit, supernaturally dwell in me, my family and their descendants, in Jesus' Name. (Isa 11:2)

DAY 29

"But the end of all things is at hand; therefore be serious and watchful in your prayers."

1 Peter 4:7

Names of Our Lord Jesus Christ:

> **Shiloh:** The scepter shall not depart from Judah, nor a lawgiver from between his feet, until Shiloh come; and unto him shall the gathering of the people be. (Genesis 49:10)

> **Son of the Blessed:** But he held his peace, and answered nothing. Again the high priest asked him, and said unto him, Art thou the Christ, the Son of the Blessed? (Mark 14:61)

> **Son of David:** The book of the generation of Jesus Christ, the son of David, the son of Abraham. (Matthew 1:1)

> **Son of God:** And was there until the death of Herod: that it might be fulfilled which was spoken of the Lord by the prophet, saying, Out of Egypt have I called my son. (Matthew 2:15)

Declarations and Confessions:

- I receive the key of the house of David, to open the door of prophecy.
- I receive the key of the house of David, to open the door of discernment of spirits.
- I receive the key of the house of David, to open the door of speaking in tongues.

➢ I receive the key of the house of David, to lockup the door of alcoholism.

➢ I receive the key of the house of David, to lockup the door of convulsions.

➢ I receive the key of the house of David, to lockup the door of principalities.

∞ I am clothed with the righteousness of God. (Job 29:14)

∞ I am safe in the protection of God. (Psalms 4:8)

❖ **Light of God,** insulate me, incubate me and consecrate me.

❖ **Fire of God,** insulate me, incubate me and consecrate me.

❖ **Blood of Jesus,** insulate me, incubate me and consecrate me.

❖ **Holy Ghost Power,** insulate me, incubate me and consecrate me.

(Scriptures: Gen. 1:3; 1:14, Dan. 3:19-25, 1 Pet. 1:2, Act. 1:8; 2:1-4)

Song of Praises:

Praises, Worship and Thanksgiving (Submit yourself to the Lord)

Prayers:

1. Almighty God, according to Your Word, I will reap what I have not labored for. Others have labored and I will enter into their labors, in the Name of Jesus. (John 4:38, Eccl. 2:26).

2. El Shaddai, God of my Strength and the Almighty God of Israel, by the power in the Covenant of Light, Holy Ghost and the Blood of Jesus: insulate me, incubate me and consecrate me, my family and their descendants, in the mighty Name of Jesus. (Acts 2:1-3)

3. My Savior, the kingdom of God is not in word, but in power. Let this power manifest in my life as I minister your Word to nations, in the Name of Jesus. (1 Corinth. 4:20)

4. King of kings, Lord of lords and Excellent Healer; protect my family, relatives and brethren from all diseases and illnesses of the land, in Jesus' Name. (Exod. 7, 8, 9, 10, 11,12)

5. My Lord Jesus, cover me with Your garment of grace and favor, each day of my life, in Jesus' Name. (Esther. 5:1-8)

6. Almighty God, anoint me for God's presence, anoint me for great battles and anoint me for conquests.

Father, anoint me to run, finish strong, and obtain the crown, in Jesus' Name. (2 Sam. 5:17-25, Jon. 2:11)

7. Almighty Father, I decree and bring forth to my destiny: the anointing for divine treasure, the anointing for divine change and the anointing for divine interpretation, in the mighty Name of Jesus. (Ps. 23:5, 2 Sam. 5:17-25)

8. Lord Jesus Christ, I receive the key to the fruit of the Spirit: love, joy, peace, longsuffering, kindness, goodness, faithfulness, gentleness and self control, in the mighty Name of Jesus. (Gal. 5:22-23)

9. LORD, the only One that can speak by fire, let your fire consume every iniquity in my hands, cleanse me from my sins and bring me closer to You, in Jesus' Name. (2 Kings 1:8-15)

10. My Heavenly Father, my destiny will not be aborted by the work of darkness and I will deliver safely, in the mighty Name of Jesus. (Luke 1:34-38)

11. Almighty God of Heaven, open my physical sight, mental sight and spiritual sight, like those two men walking with You on the road to Emmaus, in Jesus' Name. (Luke 24:12-34)

12. Lord Jesus Christ, just like Queen Esther put on her royal garment, I remove the garment of shame and

put on the garment of honor, in the mighty Name of Jesus. (Esther 5:1)

13. Holy Spirit, clothe me with the garment of the Holy Ghost, in the mighty Name of Jesus. (Esther 5:1. Acts 2:1-3)

14. Almighty God, remove every tree of limitation residing over my destiny and ministry, today, in the mighty Name of Jesus. (John 1:43-50)

15. Creator of heaven and earth and all that are in them; renew my strength and I shall mount up with wings like eagles; I will run and not be weary; and I shall walk and not faint, in the mighty Name of Jesus. (Isa. 40:31)

16. LORD, strengthen my hands, my knees and my fearful heart to receive boldness. My God will come with a vengeance and save me, in the mighty Name of Jesus. (Isa. 35:3-4)

17. Lord God, through prayer, I ask for the anointing to bring forth the needs of brethren in mysteries, and bring it to manifestation through the power of the Holy Spirit, in Jesus' Name. (Isa. 11:2)

18. My Father, keep my household from eating the bread of affliction, in Jesus' Name. (1 Kings 22:27)

19. My Father, keep my household from eating the bread of adversity, in Jesus' Name. (Isa. 30:20)

20. My Father, keep my household from eating the bread of sorrow, in Jesus' Name. (Ps. 127:2b)

21. MY Father, keep my household from eating the bread of idleness, in Jesus' Name. (Prov. 31:27)

22. My Father, keep my household from eating the bread of wickedness, in Jesus' Name. (Prov. 4:17)

23. My Father, keep my household from drinking the water of affliction, in Jesus' Name. (1 King 22:27)

24. My Father, keep my household from drinking the wine of violence, in Jesus' Name. (Prov. 4:17)

DAY 30

"But you, beloved, building yourself up on your most holy faith, praying in the Holy Spirit, keep yourselves in the love of God, looking for the mercy of our Lord Jesus unto eternal life.
And on some have compassion, making a distinction; but others save with fear, pulling them out of the fire, hating even the garment defiled by the flesh."

Jude 1:20-23

Names of Our Lord Jesus Christ:

> **Son of the Highest**: He shall be great, and shall be called the Son of the Highest: and the Lord God shall give unto him the throne of his father David. (Luke 1:32)

> **Sun of Righteousness:** But unto you that fear my name shall the Sun of righteousness arise with healing in his wings; and ye shall go forth, and grow up as calves of the stall. (Malachi 4:2)

> **True Light:** That was the true Light, which lighteth every man that cometh into the world. (John 1:9)

> **True Vine:** I am the true vine, and my Father is the husbandman. (John 15:1)

Declarations and Confessions:

- I receive the key of the house of David, to open the door to interpretation of tongues.
- I receive the key of the house of David, to Psalm 91.
- I receive the key of the house of David, to open the door of divine birth.

> I receive the key of the house of David, to lockup the door of principalities and powers.

> I receive the key of the house of David, to lockup the door of the rulers of darkness.

➢ I receive the key of the house of David, to lockup the door of hosts of wickedness.

∞ I am secure in the love of God. (Jeremiah 31:3)

∞ I am preserved by God. (Psalms 16:10)

❖ **Light of God,** insulate me, incubate me and consecrate me.

❖ **Fire of God,** insulate me, incubate me and consecrate me.

❖ **Blood of Jesus,** insulate me, incubate me and consecrate me.

❖ **Holy Ghost Power,** insulate me, incubate me and consecrate me.

(Scriptures: Gen. 1:3; 1:14, Dan. 3:19-25, 1 Pet. 1:2, Act. 1:8; 2:1-4)

Song of Praises:

Praises, Worship and Thanksgiving (Submit yourself to the Lord)

Prayers:

1. Jesus of Nazareth, endow me with Your gift of teaching, to make disciples of all nations, baptizing them in the name of Father, Son and Holy Spirit. Let them remain with you to the end, in mighty Name of Jesus. (Matt. 28:18-20)

2. Father, according to Your covenant, I'm blessed in the city and blessed in the country and my children are many. I will harvest large crops, my livestock will have many young and I will have plenty to eat. Thank You Lord, that my daily work will succeed as I claim total victory over my enemies and I am one of God's own special people. I decree and declare rain will come at the right time for me. I will lend money to many nations and not borrow. I am the head and not the tail, in the mighty Name of Jesus. (Deut. 28:1-14)

3. Almighty God, I receive Your power against principalities, powers and rulers of the darkness of this age and spiritual hosts of wickedness in high places, in the mighty Name of Jesus. (Eph. 6:12)

4. Jehovah Tsidkenu, the Righteous One, I ask for the gift of healing and miracles. Lord give me the power and anointing to heal all: demonic diseases, blindness, deafness, dumbness, lameness, cancer, aids, drunk-

enness, drug addictions, blood diseases, fibroids and barrenness, all for the expansion of Your kingdom, in the mighty Name of Jesus. (Acts 3:1-10)

5. LORD, cover me with Your garment of goodness and mercy each day of my life, in Jesus' Name. (Ps. 23:6, Deut. 28:1-14)

6. Jehovah Nissi, the Lord my Banner, I decree and declare to bring forth into my destiny the anointing for divine treasure; the anointing for divine change; the anointing for divine conquest; and the anointing of divine interpretation, in mighty Name of Jesus. (Ps. 23:5)

7. Almighty God, I receive the keys to be a problem solver for Your glory, in Jesus' Name. (Matt. 16:19, Isa. 22:22)

8. LORD, as You did to Moses, the Israelis couldn't look at his face. Shine Your everlasting light on me. LORD, insulate me, incubate me and consecrate me with Your Light, in the Name of Jesus. (Exod. 34:33-35, Dan. 3:23-25)

9. Jehovah Tsidkenu, the Lord is my Righteousness and my Heavenly Father. Remove every evil fig tree that represents limitation in my life and catapult me to the place of my destiny this month, in the mighty Name of Jesus. (John 1:44-51)

10. Lion of Judah, I decree and declare that every destiny manipulator and attacker over my life, orchestrated by the power of darkness; let the earthquakes of heaven open the ground and swallow them all now, in the Name of Jesus. (Num 16:32, 1 Sam. 14:15, 1 King 19:11, Amos 1:1, Zech. 14:5)

11. My Father in Heaven, open my eyes like you did for ancient men like: Abraham, Joseph, David, Isaiah, Ezekiel, Jeremiah, Elijah, Elisha, Daniel, Paul and John, in the mighty Name of Jesus. (Rev. 1:9-11)

12. Jehovah Nissi, the Lord is my Banner. I decree, according to your scripture in Psalm 91, these covenantal prayers will work for me, my family and my descendants, in the Name of Jesus. (Ps. 91:1-16)

13. My Lord, by the power in the Blood of Jesus, I speak supernatural healing to all organs in my body, in the mighty Name of Jesus. (Mark 11:12-20)

14. Creator of all body parts, I speak supernatural healing to all systems in my body: nervous, reproductive, digestive, respiratory, endocrine, excretory, skeletal, circulatory, and muscular, in the mighty Name of Jesus. (Mark 11:12-20)

15. My Lord, by the power in the Blood of Jesus, I speak supernatural healing to my body: head, eyes, ears,

nose, mouth, arms, hands, abdomen, legs, feet, and heart, in the mighty Name of Jesus. (Mark 11:12-20)

16. My Savior, I decree, according to Your scripture in John 17, let these covenantal prayers of Jesus work for me, my family and my descendants, in the Name of Jesus. (John 17: 1-26)

17. Lord Jesus I thank You. You have removed me from great tribulation and washed my robes and made them white in the Blood of the Lamb. (Rev. 7:14)

18. El Olam, Everlasting GOD; according to Your Word in the books of Exodus and Revelation, I will not see hunger and thirst anymore. The sun will not strike me, nor any heat in my life. The Lamb, whom is on the throne of my life, will shepherd me. The Lamb will lead me to living fountains of waters. The Almighty God will wipe away all tears from my eyes, in the mighty Name of Jesus. (Rev. 7:16-17, Exod. 15:27)

19. Ancients of Days, I thank you for the new heaven and new earth You have created for me. LORD, let Your Kingdom come and overshadow me, in all aspects of my life. For me and my offspring, the former will not be remembered anymore. By the power of the Almighty God, I shall build houses and inhabit them. I shall plant vineyards and eat their fruit. I shall not build houses and others inhabit them anymore. I shall not

plant crops and others eat them. As the days of a tree, so shall be the days of my life and descendants. I shall long enjoy the works of my hands. I shall not labor in vain nor bring forth children for trouble. I shall be a descendant of the blessed, of the LORD. I believe our Good God shall make it come to pass. Before I call Him, He will answer me. While I am still speaking, He will hear me.

The wolf and lamb shall feed together. Lions shall eat straw like an ox and so dust shall be the serpent's food. I shall not hurt nor destroy in all God's Holy Mountain, in the mighty Name of Jesus. (Isa. 65:17-25)

DAY 31

"Now when He had taken the scroll, the four living creatures and the twenty-four elders fell down before the lamb,
each having a harp and golden bowls full of incense,
which are the prayers of the saints."

Revelation 5:8

Names of Our Lord Jesus Christ:

> ➤ **Truth:** And the Word was made flesh, and dwelt among us, (and we beheld his glory, the glory as of the only begotten of the Father,) full of grace and truth. (John 1:14)

> ➤ **Witness:** Behold, I have given him for a witness to the people, a leader and commander to the people. (Isaiah 55:4)

> ➤ **Word:** In the beginning was the Word, and the Word was with God, and the Word was God. (John 1:1)

> ➤ **Word of God:** And he was clothed with vesture dipped in blood: and his name is called The Word of God. (Revelation 19:13)

Declarations and Confessions:

- I receive the key of the house of David, to open the door of the book of Genesis 12:2-3.
- I receive the key of the house of David, to open the door of the book of Deuteronomy 28:1-14.
- I receive the key of the house of David, to open the door of the book of Isaiah 11:2-3.

> ➤ I receive the key of the house of David, to lockup the door of enchantments and false visions.

➢ I receive the key of the house of David, to lockup the door of lies, terror and self deception.

➢ I receive the key of the house of David, to lockup the door of torment and Deuteronomy 28:16-44.

∞ I am with God. (Romans 8:31)

∞ I am transformed by God. (Romans 12:2)

❖ **Light of God,** insulate me, incubate me and consecrate me.

❖ **Fire of God,** insulate me, incubate me and consecrate me.

❖ **Blood of Jesus,** insulate me, incubate me and consecrate me.

❖ **Holy Ghost Power,** insulate me, incubate me and consecrate me.

(Scriptures: Gen. 1:3; 1:14, Dan. 3:19-25, 1 Pet. 1:2, Act. 1:8; 2:1-4)

Song of Praises:

Praises, Worship and Thanksgiving (Submit yourself to the Lord)

Prayers:

1. Adonai, LORD of all and my Lord Jesus, every miracle You performed on earth, count me worthy to do the same and more in Your kingdom, in the name of Jesus. (Matt. 16:19,18:18)

2. Jehovah M'qaddishkhem, my LORD, let Your covenant of salt forever be established in my life, my family's life and their descendants, in Jesus' Name. (Num. 18:19)

3. Jehovah GOD, the Lord my Sanctifier, sanctify me completely. May my spirit, my soul and my body be preserved and blameless at the coming of our Lord Jesus Christ, in Jesus' Name. (1 Thess. 5:23)

4. Jehovah Sabbaoth, the Lord of Hosts, by Your priceless Blood, insulate me, incubate me and consecrate me. Keep me by Your Blood from, principalities, powers, rulers of the darkness of this age and spiritual hosts of wickedness in heavenly places, in the mighty Name of Jesus. (Eph. 6:12)

5. Jehovah Nakeh, the GOD who smites, every destructive mountain ahead of me. Father stretch out Your mighty hand and roll down this mountain and burn it all to ashes, in the Name of Jesus. (Jer. 51:25).

6. Adonai, Lord of All, I pray according to Psalm 91and Isaiah 60 and is working for me and my family, in the mighty Name of Jesus. (Ps. 91, Isa. 60)

7. Holy Ghost and Fire, everything on earth, above and below challenging my destiny, let Your earthquakes of heaven open the ground now and swallow them all up, in the Name of Jesus. (Matt. 27:54; 28:2, Acts 16:26, Rev. 11:13)

8. Yahweh, I receive the key as a badge of power and authority to work in Your vineyard, bringing souls into Your kingdom and glorifying Your Holy Name, in the mighty Name of Jesus. (Matt. 16:18-19)

9. Alpha and Omega, reveal to me the first mystery of the Kingdom of heaven, in Jesus' Name. (Matt. 13:3-50)

10. Father, reveal to me the second mystery of Israel's blindness during this age, in Jesus' Name. (Rom. 11:25)

11. Ancient of days, reveal to me the third mystery of the translation, of the living saints at the end of this age, in Jesus' Name. (1 Corinth. 15:51-52, 1Thess. 4:13-17)

12. Father, reveal to me the fourth mystery of the New Testament Church, as one body, in Jesus' Name. (Eph. 3:1-2, Rom. 16:25)

13. My Creator, reveal to me the fifth mystery of the church as the bride of Christ, in Jesus' Name. (Eph. 5:23- 32)

14. Father, reveal to me the sixth mystery of the in-dwelling Christ, in Jesus' Name. (Gal. 2:20; Col. 1:26-27; Matt. 13:11)

15. My Lord, reveal to me the seventh mystery of God and of Christ, in Jesus' Name. (1 Corinth. 2:7, Col. 2:2, 9)

16. Lord Jesus, reveal to me the mystery of the process in which godliness is restored to man, in Jesus' Name. (1 Tim. 3:26)

17. Father, reveal to me the mystery of the seven stars and of Babylon, in Jesus' Name. (Rev. 1:20; 17:5, 7, Matt. 13:11)

18. LORD, my Father feed my household with the Bread of Life, in Jesus' Name. (John 6:35).

19. Yahweh Nissi, the LORD who is our banner. Send out by fire, four winds from Your four quarters of heaven to scatter: mountains, valleys, winds of sorrow, calamity, shame and lack; working against my destiny, in the mighty Name of Jesus. (Jer. 49:36)

20. Yahweh Jireh, the LORD who is our provider. My Father feed my household with Your Living Bread, in Jesus' Name. (John 6:41-51)

21. LORD and my Father, feed my household with Your Living Water, in Jesus' Name. (John 4:10-14)

22. Yahweh Shalom, is the LORD of Peace. I pray my God and my Everlasting Door, let me be a partaker of

these ancient blessings attached to all builders and repairers of the walls of the: Sheep Gate, Fish Gate, Old Gate, Valley Gate, Refuse Gate and Fountain Gate, in mighty Name of Jesus. (Neh. 3:1- 16, Ps. 24:7-10)

23. Yahweh Sabbaoth, the LORD of Host, I pray please answer my prayers in the day of trouble. God of Jacob let Your Name defend me. My Father, send help from Your sanctuary and strengthen me out of Zion. Father, remember all my offerings and accept my burnt sacrifices. Lord God, grant me according to my heart's desire and fulfill Your purpose in me. I rejoice in my salvation and breakthrough. May the LORD fulfill all my petitions, in the mighty Name of Jesus. (Ps 20:1-5)

24. Ancients of Days, I thank you for the new heaven and new earth You have created for me. LORD, let Your Kingdom come and overshadow me, in all aspects of my life. For me and my offspring, the former will not be remembered anymore. By the power of the Almighty God, I shall build houses and inhabit them. I shall plant vineyards and eat their fruit. I shall not build houses and others inhabit them anymore. I shall not plant crops and others eat them. As the days of a tree, so shall be the days of my life and descendants. I shall long enjoy the works of my hands. I shall not labor in

vain nor bring forth children for trouble. I shall be a descendant of the blessed, of the LORD. I believe our Good God shall make it come to pass. Before I call Him, He will answer me. While I am still speaking, He will hear me.

The wolf and lamb shall feed together. Lions shall eat straw like an ox and so dust shall be the serpent's food. I shall not hurt nor destroy in all God's Holy Mountain, in the mighty Name of Jesus. (Isa. 65:17-25)

DECLARATION AND CONFESSION PRAYERS

"This book of the Law shall not depart from your mouth, but you shall meditate in it day and night, that you may observe to do according to all that is written in it. For then you will make your way prosperous, and then you will have good success."

Joshua 1:8

Declaration and Confession Prayers
Isaiah 22:22, Matthew 7:7-8, Matthew 16:19, Revelation 3:7-8

I Receive the Key of House of David to Close and Lockup Doors:

1 Close and lockup the Door of All Sin.
2 Close and lockup the Door of Bitterness.
3 Close and lockup the Door of Bondage.
4 Close and lockup the Door of Carousing.
5 Close and lockup the Door of Covetousness.
6 Close and lockup the Door of Demons.
7 Close and lockup the Door of Depravity.
8 Close and lockup the Door of Disease.
9 Close and lockup the Door of Disobedience.
10 Close and lockup the Door of Disregard for Others.
11 Close and lockup the Door of Dissensions.
12 Close and lockup the Door of Drunkenness.
13 Close and lockup the Door of Envy.
14 Close and lockup the Door of Evil Spirits.
15 Close and lockup the Door of Excessiveness.
16 Close and lockup the Door of Factions.
17 Close and lockup the Door of Galatians 5:19.
18 Close and lockup the Door of Gluttony.
19 Close and lockup the Door of Gossip.
20 Close and lockup the Door of Greed.

I Receive the Key of House of David to Open the Doors:

1 Open the Door of Anointing.
2 Open the Door of Apostolic Gifts.
3 Open the Door of Blessings.
4 Open the Door of Deliverance.
5 Open the Door of Discernment.
6 Open the Door of Pleasing God.
7 Open the Door of Imitating God.
8 Open the Door of Encounters with God.
9 Open the Door of Encounters with Jesus.
10 Open the Door of Encounters with Holy Spirit.
11 Open the Door of Encouragement.
12 Open the Door of Endurance.
13 Open the Door of Evangelism.
14 Open the Door of Faith.
15 Open the Door of Faithfulness.
16 Open the Door of Favor.
17 Open the Door of Gentleness.
18 Open the Door of Giving.
19 Open the Door of Glory.
20 Open Door of God to Crucify my Flesh.

21	Close and lockup the Door of hostility.	21	Open the Door of Goodness.
22	Close and lockup the Door of Hypocrisy.	22	Open the Door of Greatness.
23	Close and lockup the Door of Idolatry.	23	Open the Door of Super-Natural Healing.
24	Close and lockup the Door of Immorality.	24	Open the Door of Hearing from God.
25	Close and lockup the Door of Impatience.	25	Open the Door of Holiness.
26	Close and lockup the Door of Improvidence.	26	Open the Door of Unspeakable Joy.
27	Close and lockup the Door of Impurity.	27	Open the Door of Kindness.
28	Close and lockup the Door of Infirmity.	28	Open the Door of Inspiration of God.
29	Close and lockup the Door of Jealousy.	29	Open the Door of Knowledge.
30	Close and lockup the Door of Carelessness	30	Open the Door of the Light of God.
31	Close and lockup the Door of Lack.	31	Open the Door of Longsuffering.
32	Close and lockup the Door of Laziness.	32	Open the Door of Love.
33	Close and lockup the Door of the Love of Money.	33	Open the Door of Praise.
34	Close and lockup the Door of Stinginess.	34	Open the Door of Obedience.
35	Close and lockup the Door of Murder.	35	Open the Door of Opportunities.
36	Close and lockup the Door of Anger/ Outbursts.	36	Open the Door of an Oracle
37	Close and lockup the Door of Hedonism.	37	Open the Door of Pastoral Gifts.
38	Close and lockup the Door of Poverty.	38	Open the Door of Patience.
39	Close and lockup the Door of Powers of Darkness.	39	Open the Door of Peace.
40	Close and lockup the Door of Pride.	40	Open the Door of Supernatural Power.
41	Close and lockup the Door of Ridicule.	41	Open the Door of Prophetic Gifts.

42   Close and lockup the Door of Selfish rivalries.

42   Open the Door of Supernatural Prosperity.

43   Close and lockup the Door of Selfishness.

43   Open the Door of Scriptures.

44   Close and lockup the Door of Sexual immorality.

44   Open the Door of Seeing God.

45   Close and lockup the Door of Shame.

45   Open the Door of Self Control.

46   Close and lockup the Door of Sickness.

46   Open the Door of Service to God.

47   Close and lockup the Door of Slander.

47   Open the Door of Self Sacrifice to God.

48   Close and lockup the Door of Slovenliness.

48   Open the Door of the Aroma of God.

49   Close and lockup the Door of Sorcery.

49   Open the Door of the Gift of Teaching.

50   Close and lockup the Door of Strife.

50   Open the Door of Understanding.

51   Close and lockup the Door of Drinking Alcohol.

51   Open the Door of Walking with God.

52   Close and lockup the Door of Stubbornness.

52   Open the Door of Wealth-Supernaturally.

53   Close and lockup the Door of Uncontrolled Habits.

53   Open the Door of Wisdom.

54   Close and lockup the Door of Unwise Speech.

54   Open the Door of Words of God.

55   Close and lockup the Door of Worldly Worship.

55   Open the Door of Worshipping The Creator.

56   Close and lockup the Door of satanic Dreams.

56   Open the Door of Perpetual Power.

57   Close and lockup the Door of Filthy Imaginations.

57   Open the Door of Prophetic Prayer.

58   Close and lockup the Door of Filthy Conversations.

58   Open the Door of the Prophetic Office.

59   Close and lockup the Door of Condemnation.

59   Open the Door of Prophetic Operations.

60   Close and lockup the Door of Guilt.

60   Open the Door of Prophetic Preaching.

61   Close and lockup the Door of Shame.

61   Open the Door of Prophetic Projects.

62   Close and lockup the Door of a Perverse Heart.

62   Open the Door of Prophetic Discernment.

63	Close and lockup the Door of Filthy Dreams.	63	Open the Door of the Prophetic Sphere.
64	Close and lockup the Door of an Unclean Spirit.	64	Open the Door of Prophetic Domination.
65	Close and lockup the Door of Occult Sex.	65	Open the Door of Prophetic Teaching.
66	Close and lockup the Door of Lust.	66	Open the Door of Prophetic Visions.
67	Close and lockup the Door of Promiscuity.	67	Open the Door of Prophetic Warfare.
68	Close and lockup the Door of Lasciviousness.	68	Open the Door of Prophetic Watchcare.
69	Close and lockup the Door of Prostitution.	69	Open the Door of Prophetic Wisdom.
70	Close and lockup the Door of Sexual Perversions.	70	Open the Door of Prophetic Economy.
71	Close and lockup the Door of the Spirit of Compromise	71	Open the Door of the Prophetic Mantle.
72	Close and lockup the Door of Mental Illness.	72	Open the Door of Prophetic Dreams.
73	Close and lockup the Door of Unreasonable Behaviors.	73	Open the Door of Open Visions.
74	Close and lockup the Door of Impotence.	74	Open the Door of Discipleship.
75	Close and lockup the Door of satanic Traps.	75	Open the Door of the Spirit of God.
76	Close and lockup the Door of an Evil Inheritance.	76	Open the Door of the Abrahamic Covenant.
77	Close and lockup the Door of Depression.	77	Open the Door of Being Right with God.
78	Close and lockup the Door of Bareness.	78	Open the Door of Freedom in Christ.
79	Close and lockup the Door of Premature Aging.	79	Open the Door of Reading Scriptures.
80	Close and lockup the Door of Personality Disorders.	80	Open the Door of Comfort in Christ Jesus.
81	Close and lockup the Door of Mental Blindness.	81	Open the Door of Wisdom in the LORD.
82	Close and lockup the Door of Pain Killers.	82	Open the Door of the Word of knowledge.
83	Close and lockup the Door of Drug Abuse.	83	Open the Door of Faith.

84 Close and lockup the Door of Mental Dullness.

84 Open the Door of Healings.

85 Close and lockup the Door of Premature Death.

85 Open the Door of Working Miracles.

86 Close and lockup the Door of Alcoholism.

86 Open the Door of Prophecies.

87 Close and lockup the Door of Convulsions.

87 Open the Door of Discerning of Spirits.

88 Close and lockup the Door of Principalities.

88 Open the Door of Speaking in Tongues.

89 Close and lockup the Door of Leviathan Power.

89 Open the Door of Interpretations of Tongues.

90 Close and lockup the Door to Rulers of Darkness.

90 Open the Door of Psalm 91.

91 Close and lockup the Door to Hosts of Wickedness.

91 Open the Door of Divine Birth.

92 Close and lockup the Door of Spiritual Sanitation.

92 Open the Door of Genesis 12:2-3.

93 Close and lockup the Door of Enchantments.

93 Open the Door of Deuteronomy 28:1-14.

94 Close and lockup the Door of False Visions.

94 Open the Door of the Spirit of the Lord.

95 Close and lockup the Door of Lies.

95 Open the Door of the Spirit of Wisdom.

96 Close and lockup the Door of Religion.

96 Open the Door of the Spirit of Understanding.

97 Close and lockup the Door of Household Wickedness.

97 Open the Door of the Spirit of Counsel.

98 Close and lockup the Door of Self Deception.

98 Open the Door of the Spirit of Might.

99 Close and lockup the Door of Terror, Torment, Despair.

99 Open the Door of the Spirit of Knowledge.

100 Close and lockup the Door of Deuteronomy 28:16-44.

100 Open the Door of the Fear of the Lord.

PROSPERITY AND WEALTH SCRIPTURES

"And you shall remember the LORD your God, for it is He who gives you power to get wealth, that He may establish His covenant which He swore to your fathers, as it is this day."

Deuteronomy 8:18

"Save now, I pray, O LORD; O LORD, I pray, send now prosperity."

Psalm 118:25

PROSPERITY AND WEALTH SCRIPTURES

LORD God, I claim the wealth of this earth, to expand the Kingdom of God and the wealth of my descendants, for it all belongs to the Lord Jesus Christ. I claim everything that Jesus' death has made available for me, therefore I receive and I decree it in the Name of Jesus. I command you devil to loose the wealth of this earth and I grab it in the name of Jesus. I command you satan, take your hands off the wealth and prosperity of my inheritance and nations now, in Jesus Name. I command now, in the name of Jesus, every hindering force against me and my wealth to stop now. By the Blood of Jesus, devil I bind you and render you ineffective against me and my family in, Jesus' Name. Jesus is Lord of this earth, and the earth and its fullness belong to Him. As a joint heir with Jesus, I claim the wealth of this earth. I command wealth to come to me now, in the Name of Jesus. *Save now, I pray,*

O LORD, O LORD, I pray. Send prosperity to me now, in the Name of Jesus! (Psalm 118:25)

Genesis 12:2	I am a great nation.
Genesis 12:2	I am blessed.
Genesis 12:2	My name shall be great.
Genesis 12:3	I will be a blessing to others and nations.
Genesis 12:3	Those who bless me, will be blessed.
Genesis 12:3	Almighty God will curse those who curse me
Genesis12:3	In me, all the families of the earth shall be blessed.
Exodus 23:20	Almighty God is enemy to my enemies and He is an adversary to my adversaries.
Deuteronomy 1:11	My LORD God of my father will make me a thousand times more numerous than my father, and bless me as He has promised.
Deuteronomy 8:18	I remember the Lord my God, for it is He that has given me the power to get wealth.
Deuteronomy 28:3	My cities and farms will be successful.

Deuteronomy 28:4	I will produce many children and they will be blessed.
Deuteronomy 28:4	I will harvest large crops.
Deuteronomy 28:4	My livestock is fruitful.
Deuteronomy 28:5	I have plenty to eat.
Deuteronomy 28:6	My daily work will be successful.
Deuteronomy 28:10	By the reason of anointing of God, I am able to defeat my enemies.
Deuteronomy 28:10	I am God's own special people.
Deuteronomy 28:12	Rain will come at the right times for me and my children and their descendants.
Deuteronomy 28:12	I have plenty of money to lend to others and to nations.
Deuteronomy 28:13	My nation will be a leader among nations.
Deuteronomy 28:13	My nation will be wealthy and powerful.
Leviticus 26:4	Rain will come in its season for me.
Leviticus 26:4	My land shall yield its produce and the trees of the field shall yield their fruit.
Leviticus 26:5	My threshing shall last till the time of vintage, and the vintage shall last till

the time of sowing. I will have plenty to eat.

Leviticus 26:5   I will eat my bread to the full, and dwell in my land safely.

Leviticus 26:6   I will have peace and live in peace in my land.

Leviticus 26:6   I will rest without fear and no one will make me afraid.

Leviticus 26:7   I will have protection from wild animals and enemies.

Leviticus 26:8   I will chase after my enemies and they shall fall by the sword before me and I will defeat all my enemies.

Leviticus 26:9   Five of me will chase hundred, and a hundred of me will put ten thousand to flight. My nation shall grow strong.

Leviticus 26:11   God is dwelling among us, and He walk with us.

Psalm 1:3   I am like a tree that's planted by the rivers of water. Everything I do will prosper and flourish.

Psalm 20:1   The LORD will answer me in the day of trouble.

Psalm 20:1   The Name of the God of Jacob will defend me.

Psalm 20:2	Almighty God will send help from sanctuary for me.
Psalm 20:2	The LORD will strengthen me out of Zion.
Psalm 20:3	My Lord will remember all my offerings and accept my burnt sacrifice.
Psalm 20:4	My Lord will grant me according to my heart's desires and fulfill my purpose.
Psalm 20:5	We will rejoice in my salvation in the mighty Name of Jesus.
Psalm 20:5	The Name of my God will set up my banners.
Psalm 20:5	My LORD will fulfill ALL my petitions.
Psalm 23:5	The Lord prepared a table before me in the presence of my enemies. He anoints my head with oil, my cup running over.
Psalm 34:8-10	I am blessed because I trust in the Lord and I reverence the Lord. Therefore there is no want in my life. The young lions do lack and suffer hunger; but I shall not want any good thing.

Psalm 35:27	I shout for joy; Let the Lord be magnified, which hath pleasure in the prosperity of His servant.
Psalm 37:4	I delight myself in the Lord, and He gives me the desires of my heart.
Psalm 37: 18-19	My inheritance shall be forever. I shall not be ashamed in the evil time; and in the days of famine, I shall be satisfied.
Psalm 112:1-3	I delight myself in the Word of the Lord, therefore, I am blessed. Wealth and riches shall be in my house and my righteousness endureth forever.
Proverb 8:18	With me are riches and honor, enduring wealth and prosperity.
Proverb 8:21	My love for the Lord God is great, He has endowed me to inherit wealth and He will fill my treasuries.
Proverb 10:22	The blessing of the Lord makes me rich and He adds no trouble to it.
Proverb 13:22	The wealth of the sinner is laid up for me.
Proverb 14:24	I am crowned with wealth.
Ecclesiastes 5:19	I receive wealth from the Lord and the good health to enjoy it.

Ecclesiastes 2:26	The LORD has given me His wisdom and knowledge and joy. He has removed from me, the spirit of sinner; work of gathering and collecting.
Ecclesiastes 5:19	LORD God had given me riches and wealth, and power to eat of it. I receive my heritage and I rejoice in my labor, this gift of God to me.
Isaiah 10:27	All burdens shall be taken from my shoulders, and every yoke taken off my neck. Every yoke shall be destroyed because of the anointing.
Luke 6:38	I have given and it shall be given unto me, good measure, pressed down, shaken together, and running over, will men give unto my bosom. For with the same measure that I use it shall be measured back to me.
Mark 11:24	What things soever I desire, when I pray, I believe that I have receive them and I shall have them.
Luke 12:31	I seek first the kingdom of God and His righteousness, therefore every-thing I need shall be added unto me.

John 4:38	Lord Jesus, that which I have not labored, others have labored and I have entered into their labors.
John 16:23	Whatsoever I ask the Father in the name of His Son Jesus, He will give it to me.
2 Corinthians 8:9	I know the grace of my Lord Jesus Christ, that, though He was rich, yet for my sake He became poor, that through His poverty I might be rich.
2 Corinthians 9:8	God is able to make all grace abound toward me; that I always having sufficiency in all things; and have an abundance for every good work.
Galatians 3:14	In Christ Jesus, Abraham's blessing are mine.
Galatians 6:9	I will not grow weary, in due time and at the appointed season, I shall reap, I will not lose heart.
Philippians 4:19	My God supplies all of my need according to His riches in glory by Christ Jesus.
3 John 2	I am prospering in every way. My body keeps well, even as my soul keeps well and prospers.

Revelation 2:17	Lord Jesus, I am an over-comer; I receive some of the hidden manna to eat and my name is written on the white stone.
Revelation 22:2	Lord Jesus, the tree of life bring forth twelve fruits for me and each tree yielding its fruit every month. The leaves of the tree will heal me and my nation.

HEALTH AND HEALING SCRIPTURES

"But He was wounded for our transgressions, He was bruised for our iniquities: the chastisement of our peace was upon Him; and with His stripes we are healed"

Isaiah 53:5

HEALTH AND HEALING SCRIPTURES

T he Word of God never fails, just have faith in His Word. As we go through challenges of life or confront a stubborn situation, especially in area of health, the only weapon we need is loudly declaring the Word of God.

1. And said, If you diligently heed to the voice of the LORD Your God and do what is right in His sight, give ear to His commandments and keep His statutes, *I will put none of the diseases on you which I have brought on the Egyptians: For I am the LORD that heals you.* (Exod. 15:26)

2. So Moses cried out to the LORD, saying, "*Please heal her, O God, I pray!*" (Num. 12:13)

3. Now see that I, even I, am He, And there is no God besides Me; I kill and *make alive*; *Nor is there any who can deliver from My hand.* (Deut. 32:39)

4. Then he went out to the source of the water, and cast in the salt there, and said, "Thus says the LORD: '*I have healed this water; from it there shall be no more death and barrenness.*'" (2 Kings 2:21)

5. "If My people who are called by My name will humble themselves, and pray and seek My face, and turn from their wicked ways, *then I will hear from heaven, and will forgive their sin, and heal their land.* (2 Chron. 7:14)

6. And the LORD listened to Hezekiah, *and healed the people.* (2 Chron. 30:20)

7. Have mercy on me, O LORD, for I am weak: O LORD, *heal* me; for my bones are troubled. My soul also is greatly troubled: But You, O LORD, how long? (Ps. 6:2-3)

8. O LORD my God, I cried out to You, and You *healed* me. (Ps. 30:2)

9. I said, LORD, be merciful to me; *Heal* my soul, for I have sinned against You. (Ps. 41:4)

10. You have made the earth tremble; You have broken it; *Heal* its breaches, for it is shaking. (Ps. 60:2)

11. Who forgives all your *iniquities*, Who *heals* all your diseases. (Ps. 103:3)

12. He sent His Word, and *healed* them, and delivered them from their destructions. (Ps. 107:20)

13. I shall not die, *but live*, And declare the works of the LORD. (Ps. 118:17)

14. He *heals* the brokenhearted and binds up their wounds. (Ps. 147:3)

15. I will be *health* to your flesh, And strength to your bones. (Prov. 3:8)

16. For they are life to those that find them, and *health* to all their flesh. (Prov. 4:22)

17. There is one who speaks like the piercings of a sword, But the tongue of the wise promotes *health*. (Prov. 12:18)

18. A wicked messenger falls into trouble, But a faithful ambassador brings *health*. (Prov. 13:17)

19. Pleasant words are like a honeycomb, Sweetness to the soul, and *health* to the bones. (Prov. 16:24)

20. A time to kill, and *a time to heal*; a time to break down, and *a time to build up*. (Eccl.. 3:3)

21. Moreover the light of the moon will be as the light of the sun, and the light of the sun shall be sevenfold, as the light of seven days, in the day that the LORD binds up the bruise of His people, and *heals* the stroke of their wound. (Isa. 30:26)

22. But He was wounded for our transgressions, He was bruised for our iniquities: The chastisement of

our peace was upon Him; and by His stripes we are *healed*. (Isa. 53:5)

23. I have seen his ways, and will *heal* him: I will also lead him, and restore comforts to him and to his mourners. (Isa. 57:18)

24. "I create the fruit of the lips; Peace, peace to him that is far off, and to him who is near," Says the LORD; "and I will *heal* him." (Isa. 57:19)

25. Then your light shall break forth like the morning, and your *healing* shall spring forth speedily: and your righteousness shall go before you; the glory of the LORD shall be your rear reward. (Isa. 58:8)

26. The Spirit of the LORD God is upon Me, because the LORD has anointed Me to preach good tidings to the poor; He has sent Me to *heal the brokenhearted*, to proclaim liberty to the captives, and the opening of the prison to those who are bound. (Isa. 61:1)

27. *Heal* me, O LORD, and I shall be *healed*; Save me, and I shall be saved, for You are my praise. (Jer. 17:14)

28. "For I will restore *health* to you and *heal* you of your wounds", says the LORD; because they called you an outcast, saying, "This is Zion, whom no one seeks her." (Jer. 30:17)

29. Behold, I will bring it *health* and *healing*; I will *heal* them, and will reveal to them the abundance of peace and truth. (Jer. 33:6)

30. Then he said to me, "This water flows toward the eastern region, goes down into the valley, and enters the sea. When it reaches the sea, its waters are *healed.*" (Ezek. 47:8-9)

31. Come, and let us return unto the LORD; for He has torn, but He will *heal* us; He has stricken, but he *will bind us up.* (Hos. 6:1)

32. I taught Ephraim to walk, taking them by their arms; but they did not know that I *healed* them. (Hos. 11:3)

33. I will *heal* their backsliding, I will love them freely, for My anger has turned away from him. (Hos.14:4-6)

34. But to you who fear My name The *Sun of Righteousness* shall arise with *healing* in His wings; And you shall go out, and grow fat like stall-fed calves. (Mal. 4:2)

35. And Jesus went about all Galilee, teaching in the synagogues, *preaching the gospel of the kingdom*, and *healing* all kinds of sickness and all kinds of disease among the people. (Matt. 4:23)

36. Now when Jesus had entered Capernaum, a centurion came to Him, pleading with Him, saying "Lord my servant is lying at home paralyzed, dreadfully tor-

mented. *And Jesus said to him, "I will come and heal him."* (Matt. 8:5-7)

37. And Jesus said to the centurion, "Go your way; and as you have believed, so let it be done for you". And his servant was *healed* that same hour. (Matt. 8:13)

38. When the evening had come, they brought to Him many who were demons possessed. And He cast out the spirits with His word, and *healed* all who were sick: (Matt 8:16)

39. And Jesus answered and said, "Suffer ye thus far." And he touched his ear, and *healed* him. (Luke 22:51)

40. And so you go preach, saying the K*ingdom of heaven is at hand. Heal the sick, cleanse the lepers, raise the dead, cast out demons,* freely you have received freely give. (Matt 10:7-8)

41. Immediately the fountain of her blood was dried up; and she felt in her body that she was *healed* of the affliction. (Mark 5:29)

42. The Spirit of the LORD is upon me, because He has anointed Me to preach the gospel to the poor; He has sent Me to *heal* the brokenhearted, to proclaim liberty to the captives, and recovery of sight to the blind, to set at liberty those who are oppressed. To proclaim the acceptable year of the LORD. (Luke 4:18-19)

43. And certain women, who had been *healed* of evil spirits and infirmities, Mary called Magdalene, out of whom had come seven devils. (Luke 8:2)

44. Then Peter said, "Silver and gold I do not have, but what I do have I give you; In the name of Jesus Christ of Nazareth, *rise up and walk.*" (Acts 3:6)

45. And Peter said to him, "Aeneas, Jesus the Christ *heals* you. Arise and make your bed." Then he arose immediately. (Acts 9:34)

46. And make straight paths for your feet, *so that what is lame may not be dislocated, but let it rather be healed.* (Heb. 12:13)

47. Confess your trespasses to one another, and pray for one another, *that you may be healed. The effective, fervent prayer of a righteous man avails much.* (James 5:16)

48. Who Himself bore our sins in His own body on the tree, that we, having died to sins, might live for righteousness: *by whose stripes you were healed.* (1 Peter 2:24)

49. Beloved, *I pray that you may prosper in all things and be in health, just as your soul prospers.* (3 John 2)

50. In the middle of its street and on either side of the river, was the tree of life, which bore twelve fruits, *each tree*

yielding its fruit every month: The leaves of the tree were for the healing of the nations. (Rev. 22:2)

ABDOMINAL	Matthew 15:21-28, Luke 7:24-30, Psalm. 30:2, Proverbs 3:7-8; 4:20-22
AFFLICTION	Psalm 44, 60, 74, 79, 80, 83, 89, 94, 102, 129, 137, Mark 5:29, 2 Corinthians 12:1-10
ARTHRITIS	Galatians 3:13-14, Job 4:3-4, Psalm 145:14;146:7-8, Proverbs 14:30; 16:24, Isaiah 35:3, Hebrew 12:12, 13
ANXEITY/FEAR	Leviticus 26:6-8, Deuteronomy 20:3-4; 31:8, Psalm 46:2
ANGER	James 1:19, Proverbs 14:17, 29; 15:18; 16:32; 19:11
ALZHEIMER	Psalm 20, 67, 122, 132, 144, 2 Chronicles 5:10
ASTHMA	Psalm 91:3, Lamentation 3:56, Joel 2:32, Acts 17:25
BED WETTING	Matthew 8:17, Psalm 25:20; 32:6; 69:15; 144:7
BLIDNESS	Matthew 9:27-31, 12:22, Mark 8:22-36; 10:46-52, John 9:1-7

BLOOD DISEASES	Mark 5:29, Psalm 138:7, Proverbs 3:5-8, Hebrew 4:12, Ezekiel 16:6, Joel 3:21, 1 Corinthians 3:16
BONES	Psalm 6:2; 32:3; 34:20, Proverbs 3:5-8; 14:30; 17:22, Isaiah 58:11, Hebrew 4:12
BROKEN HEART	Romans 15:13, Psalm 34; 42:11
CANCER	Proverbs 4:20-22, 2 Timothy 1:7, 2 Thessalonians 3:3, Matthew 15:13, Mark 11:23-24
CONFUSION	Proverbs 3:5; 14, 15
CONTRITION	Psalm 13, 22, 69, 77, 88, 143
LAMENESS	Acts 3:1-10, Luke 13:11-13, Matthew 9:2-7
DEPRESSION	Psalm 68:20
DIABETES	Psalm 103:3; 107:20; 138, Proverbs 12:18, Jeremiah 17:14a; 33:6, I Peter 3:12a, 3 John 2, James 5:16
DEAF	Psalm 91:10-11; 12:22, Mark 7:31-37, Matthew 10:8; 13:15
DUMP	Matthew 9:32-33; 10:8, 13:15
DEATH	Matthew 9:18-19; 23-25, Mark 5:22-24; 38-42, Luke 8:41-42; 49-56; 7:11-13, John. 11:1-44

DERIVED PUBLIC

WORSHIP	Psalm 42, 43, 63, 84, Ephesians 6:12-20
DEMONIC	Matthew 8:28-34; 9:32-33; 15:21-28, Mark 5:1-15; 7:24-30, Luke 8:27-35
DRINKING	Proverb 20:1; 23:20; 21, 29-35; 31:4-7, Matthew 8:28-34; 9:32-33; 15:21
EARS	Psalm 146:8a, Isaiah 29:18; 32:3; 35:5; 42:7, Matthew 11:5, 13:15, Hebrew 13:8, Job 36:15, Psalm 91:3
EMPLOYMENT	Deuteronomy 28:1-13; 30:9, Proverbs 22:4, John 4:38
EPILEPSY	Matthew 17:14-18, Mark 9:17-29, Luke 9:38-43
EYES	Psalm. 146:8, Isaiah 29:18; 32:3; 35:5; 42:7, Matthew 11:5, 13:15, Hebrew 13:8, Job 36:15, Psalm 91:3
FAMILY	I Timothy 5:8; Proverbs 13:24; 19:18; 22:6, 15; 23:13, 14
FAMINE	Matthew 14:15-21; 15:32-38, Mark 6:35-44; 8:1-9, Luke 9:12-17, John 6:5-13
FEVER:	Matthew 8:14-17, Mark 1:30-31, Luke 4:38-39.

GLUTTON	Romans 14:17, Psalm 146:7
HEADACHES	Psalm 25:18; 42:11c; 119:25; 119:50, Isaiah 57:19, John 14:27, Romans 8:11
HEART DISEASE	Psalm 27:14; 28:7; 31:24; 73:26, Proverbs 4:23; 17:22
HEARTACHE	Psalm 28:7; 34:18; 147:3, Proverbs 4:23; 15:13, Isaiah 30:15b, Jeremiah 31:13b
HEMORRHAGE	Matthew 9:20-22, Mark 5:25-29, Luke 8:43-48
INJUSTICE	Revelation 16:7, Isaiah 56:1
INTERCESSION	Psalm 20, 67, 122, 132, 144
JEALOUSY	Proverbs 3:31, 32; 6:34, 35; 14:30; 23:17; 24:1, 2, 19, 20; 27:4
LAZINESS	Proverbs 6:6-11; 10:4-5; 12:27; 13:4; 15:19; 18:9
LEPROSY/	
SKIN DISEASES	Matthew 8:2-4, Mark 1:40-42; 3:1-5, Luke 5:12-13, 14:1-4, 17:11-19
LYING SPIRIT	Proverbs 6:16-17; 10:18; 12:2, 17-19; 14:2,24; 17:4, 20; 19:22, 24, 28,29
LUST	Proverbs 6:25; 22:4, Romans 13:1-5; I Corinthians 6:9; 6:18,
MARRIAGES:	Ephesians 5:33, 1 Peter 3:7

PAIN	Psalm 4:8; 25:18; 25:20; 147:3, Isaiah 53:4, John 14:27 Proverbs 3:24
PARALYSIS	Matthew 8: 5-13; 9:2-7; 12:10-13, Mark 2:3-12; 3:1-5, Luke 5:18-25; 6:6-10
PERVERSION	Romans13:1-5; I Corinthian 6:9,18, Proverbs 6:25, 22:4
PENITENCE	Psalm 6, 32, 38, 51, 102, 130, 143
PRIDE	Proverbs 6:17; 11:2; 13:10; 15:25; 16:18-19; 18:12; 21:4, 24; 29:23, 30:13.
PRIDE/JEALOSY	Romans 13:1-5; I Corinthians 6:9,18, Proverbs 6:25; 22:4, Galatians 5:20
POISONING	Mark 16:18
REBELLION	Colossians 3: 20-2, Matthew 18:18
SATANIC SIN	Colossians 1: 13-15, 1Timohy 1 9-11
SICKNESS	Isaiah 53:5, Matthew 9:30, 1 Peter 2:24
SLEEPLESSNESS	Psalm 3:5; 4:8; 127:2, Proverbs 3:24, Ecclesiastes 5:12, Isaiah 29:10
STROKES	1 Samuel 2:4, Psalm 56:12-13; 116:8-10; 138:7; 145:14, Proverbs 3:23
SLEEPINESS	Psalm 132:4, Proverbs 20:13, Romans 13:11

TIREDNESS	Psalm138:7, Isaiah 40:29; 40:31, Matthew 8:17, Romans 8:26, 1 Corinthians 6:17, 2 Corinthians 3:6
TROUBLE	Psalm 4, 5, 11, 20, 28, 41, 55, 59, 64, 70, 109, 120, 140, 141, 143
ULCERS/WOUNDS	Psalm 147:3, Jeremiah 30:17
UNCLEAN SPIRIT	Mark 1:23-26, Luke 4:33-35, Psalm 147:3; Jeremiah 30:17
OTHERS	Psalm 30:2; 34:10,19; 55:18; 97:10b; 103:3; 119:93, Isaiah 53:4; John 8:36, Romans 8:2,32, 2 Corinthians 2:14, 1 John 3:8, 3 John 2, 1 Peter 2:24

ANCIENT PRAYERS FROM THE BIBLE

Then they took away the stone from the place where the dead man was lying. And Jesus lifted up His eyes and said,

"Father, I thank You that You have heard Me, And I know that You always hear Me, but because of the people who are standing by I said this that they may believe that You sent Me."

Now when He had said these things, He cried with a loud voice, "Lazarus, come forth"

John 11:41-42

ANCIENT PRAYERS FROM THE BIBLE

How we pray determines the kind of answers we received. Jesus taught us how to pray in Matthew 6:9 and also told us in John 17 (Christ's high priest, intercessory prayer). I believe when you study some of these ancient prayers, the Holy Spirit will magnifies His purpose in our lives and will start to pray according to the will of the Father rather than according to our needs. Let us study our ancestors' and how they prayed.

Our Lord Jesus Christ Prayers:

- **"The Lord's Prayer"**: Matthew 6:9-13, Luke 11:2-4
- **God to reveal Himself** to simple people: Matt. 11:25-36, Luke 10:21
- **The Garden of Gethsemane**: Matt. 26:36-44, Mark 14:32-39

- **Jesus prayer from the Cross**: Matt. 27:46, Mark 15:34, Luke 23: 34, 46
- **Jesus prayer raising of Lazarus:** John 11: 41-42
- **Jesus prayer facing death**: John: 12:27-28
- **Jesus prayer for His followers:** John 17

Old Testament Prayers

- **Abraham prayer** for Sodom: Genesis18:22-33
- **Abraham's prayer for guidance for his servant** : Genesis 24:12-24
- **Isaac's prayer for blessing**: Genesis 27
- **Jacob's prayer vow at Bethel**: Genesis 28
- **Jacob's desperate prayer** at Peniel: Genesis 32
- **Jacob's prayer** for blessing his sons: Genesis 48, 49
- **Moses** song of thanksgiving for deliverance from Egypt: Exodus 15
- **Moses** plea for Israel when they worshipped the golden calf: Exodus 32, Deuteronomy 9
- **Moses prayed for** asking to see God's glory: Exodus 33
- **Aaron's** blessing of prayer: Numbers 6
- **Moses** plead with God to forgive his rebellious people: Numbers 14
- **Balaam** on God's instruction, blesses Israel: Numbers 22-24
- **Moses** song God and his people: Deuteronomy 32

- **Moses** blesses the people of Israel: Deuteronomy 33
- **Joshua's** prayer after defeat at Ai: Joshua 7
- **Joshua's** prayer for time to complete his victory: Joshua 10
- **Deborah's** prayer of song of thanksgiving for victory : Judges 5
- **Gideon's** prayer for signs: Judges 6
- **Hannah's** prayer for a son: I Samuel 1; Her thanksgiving: I Samuel 2
- **Samuel's** prayer for the nation: I Samuel 7
- **David's** prayer following God's promise of a lasting succession: II Samuel 7, I Chronicles 17
- **David's** prayer of song of thanksgiving for deliverance: II Samuel 22, Psalms 18
- **Solomon's** prayer for wisdom: I Kings 3, II Chronicles 1
- **Solomon's** prayer at the dedication of the temple: I Kings 8, II Chronicles 6
- **Elijah's** prayer on Mt Carmel: I Kings 18
- **Elijah's** prayer and the gentle voice: I Kings 19
- Prayer at the time of **Sennacherib's siege**: II Kings 19, Isaiah 37
- Thanksgiving prayer as the **Ark is brought to Jerusalem**: II Chron. 17
- **David's prayer for Solomon**: II Chronicles 29
- **Ezra's** prayer of confession of the nation's sin: Ezra 9

- **Nehemiah's prayer** for his people: Nehemiah 1
- Prayer for the public **confession led by Ezra**: Nehemiah 9
- **Job's** prayer seeking the reason for his suffering: Job 10
- **Job's** prayer for pleads his case: Job 13-14
- **Job's prayer of** confession: Job 42

Prophets (Seers) Prayers:

- Prayers of **Isaiah**: Isaiah 25, 33, 63-66
- **Hezekiah's** prayer of his illness: Isaiah 38
- Prayer of **Jeremiah:** Jeremiah 11; 12; 14; 20; 32
- Prayer of **Laments** for the fall of Jerusalem: Lamentations 1-4
- Prayer for **Restoration:** Lamentations 5
- **Daniel's prayer for the King's dream**: Daniel 2
- Prayer of **Nebuchadnezzar's** praises to God: Daniel 4
- Prayer of **Daniel** at the end of the exile: Daniel 9
- Prayer of **Jonah's** disobedience: Jonah 2
- Prayer of **Habakkuk** and questions to God: Habakkuk 1
- Prayer of **Habakkuk:** Habakkuk 3

Paul (the Apostle) Prayers in the Bible:

- Prayer for the **Christians at Rome**: Romans 1:8-10
- Prayer for **Israel**: Romans 10:1

- **Church at Corinth** prayer 1 Corinthians 1:4-9, 2 Corinthians 13:7-9
- Prayer of **Thanksgiving for God's** Comfort in trouble: 2 Corinthians 1:3-4
- Prayer of **Thanksgiving for Spiritual riches in Christ**: Ephesians 1:8-14
- Prayer for the **Ephesians Christians**: Ephesians 1:16-23; 3:14-19
- Prayer for the **Philippians Christians**: Philippians 1:8-11
- Prayer for the **Church at Colosse**: Colossians1:3-14
- Prayer for the **Christians at Thessalonica**: I Thessalonians 1:2-3; 2:13; 3:9-13; 5:23
- Prayer for the **Christians at Thessalonica**: II Thessalonians 1:3; 2:13; 16-17; 3:16
- Prayer for **Timothy**: II Timothy 1:3-4
- Prayer for **Philemon**: Philemon 1: 4-6

Psalmist (David) Prayers:
- Prayer for the **evening:** Psalm 4
- Prayer for the **morning:** Psalm 5
- Prayer for the **shepherd:** Psalm 23
- Prayer for **praise and worship:** Psalm 24:67; 92, 95-98, 100,113,145,148,150
- Prayer for **guidance:** Psalm 25

- Prayer for **trust: Psalm** 37, 62
- Prayer for **deliverance:** Psalm 40, 116
- Prayer for **longing for God**: Psalm 27, 42, 63:84
- Prayer for **forgiveness:** Psalm 51, 130
- Prayer for **thanksgiving:** Psalm 65, 111, 136
- Prayer for **help in trouble**: Psalm 66, 69, 86, 88, 102, 140, 143
- Prayer for **God's constant love** and care: Psalm 89, 103, 107, 146
- Prayer for **God's majesty and glory**: Psalm 8, 29, 93, 104
- Prayer for **God's knowledge and presence**: Psalm 139
- Prayer for **God's word**: Psalm 19, 119
- Prayer for **God's protection**: 46, 91, 135
- Prayer for **David**: 2 Samuel 7:18-29

New Testament Prayers:
- Prayer of **Mary's thanksgiving**: Luke 1: 46-55
- Prayer of **Zechariah**: Luke 1:68-79
- Prayer of **Simeon**: Luke 2:29-35
- Prayer of the **Pharisee and tax collector**: Luke 18:10-13
- Prayer of the **church facing threats**: Acts 4:24-30
- Prayer of **Stephen at his death**: Acts 7:59-60
- Prayer of **Peter's thanksgiving**: I Peter 1:3-5
- Prayer of **John** for Gaius: 3 John 1:2

Covenantal Eight Prayers:

1. **Edenic Covenant Prayer**: Genesis 2:16 (Conditional covenant of man's existence)

2. **Adamic Covenant Prayer**: Genesis 3:15

3. **Nohanic Covenant Prayer**: Genesis 8:20-22; 9:16

4. **Abrahamic Covenant Prayer**: Genesis 12:2; 17:1-15; 18:1-33, John 8:39

5. **Mosaic Covenant Prayer**: Exodus 19:5

6. **Palestinian Covenant Prayer**: Deuteronomy 30:3 (final restoration and conversion of Israel)

7. **Davidic Covenant Prayer**: 2 Samuel 7:8, Matthew 1:1, Luke 1:31-33, Romans 1:3

8. **New Covenant Prayer**: Hebrews 8:8

PARABLE OF JESUS CHRIST AND KINGDOM PRAYERS

"Our Father in heaven, hallowed be Your name. Your kingdom come. Your will be done on earth as it is in heaven. Give us this day our daily bread and forgive us our debts, as we forgive our debtors. And do not lead us into temptation but deliver us from the evil one. For Yours is the kingdom and the power and the glory forever. Amen"

Matthew 6:9-13

PARABLES OF JESUS CHRIST AND KINGDOM PRAYERS

M any years ago when first inspired to write this prayer book, I was instructed by the Holy Spirit to learn and study the parables of Jesus Christ for prayer. I've since learned it's a good tool for any Christian or intercessor to use while praying, as I used most of them in this prayer book. So, I encourage reading and then asking the Holy Spirit for understanding and turning these parables into kingdom prayers. If we seek whole-heartedly those things Jesus Christ desires most, He will also do the things we do not even think to ask. Our Father always knows what is in the mind of his children and their needs.

But seek first the kingdom of God and His righteousness, and all these things shall be added to you. (Matthew 6:33)

But those who seek the Lord shall not lack any good thing. (Psalms 34:10)

Nevertheless, there is great value in studying the parables, as they illustrate some of Jesus' most important teachings. The parables of Christ demand crucial responses from us, just as they did from those who first heard them. In order to gain the greatest benefit from the parables, we must understand what they are and how they function.

Please understand that Christ's teaching and His parables focus on the Kingdom. The Kingdom in the gospels does not have to do with a physical territory, but with the rule and authority of God on earth, in the person of Christ. Jesus demonstrated that Kingdom authority over disease, demonic forces, nature, and supremely over all sin and death. In His teaching and through parables, He reveals the standards and values of the Kingdom. Unfortunately, because of our sinful nature, our minds are closed and hinder our response.

It is my prayer that you will be captivated and challenged by the parables and will have the ears to hear with understanding. Ultimately, prayers can be powerfully enhanced when turning the scripture-parables of Jesus Christ, into prayer. These are the parables captioned in this book.

1. **Cancelled Debts**: Luke 7:41-41

2. **Cost of Discipleship**: Luke 14:28-33

3. **Faithful and Wise Servant**: Matthew 24:45-5, Luke 12:42-48

4. **Fig Tree**: Matthew 24:32-35; Mark 13:28-31, Luke 21:29-33

5. **Good Samaritan**: Luke 10:30-37

6. **Great Banquet**: Luke 14:16-24

7. **Growing Seed**: Mark 4:26-29

8. **Hidden Treasure and Pearl**: Matthew 13:44-46

9. **Honor at a Banquet**: Luke 14:7-14

10. **Husbandmen**: Matthew 21:33-40, Mark 12:1-11, Luke 20: 9-18

11. **Laborers in the Vineyard**: Matthew 20:1-16

12. **Lamp under a Bushel**: Matthew 5:14-16, Mark 4:21-22, Luke 11:33-36

13. **Leaven**: Matthew 13:33, Luke 13:20-21

14. **Lost Coin**: Luke 15:8-10

15. **Lost Sheep**: Matthew 18:12-14, Luke 15:4-7

16. **Mustard Seed**: Matthew 13:31-32, Mark 4:30-32, Luke 13:18-19

17. **New Cloth on an Old Garment**: Matthew 9:16, Mark 2:21, Luke 5:36

18. **New Wine in Old Wineskins**: Matthew 9:17, Mark 2:22, Luke 5:37-39

19. **Net**: Matthew 13:47-50
20. **Obedient Servants**: Luke 17:7-10
21. **Owner of a House**: Matthew 13:52
22. **Persistent Friend**: Luke 11:5-8
23. **Persistent Widow**: Luke 18:2-8
24. **Pharisee Friend and the Publican**: Luke 18:10-14
25. **Prodigal (Lost) Son**: Luke 15:11-32
26. **Rich Fool**: Luke 12:16-21
27. **Rich Man and Lazarus**: Luke 16:19-31
28. **Sheep and Goats**: Matthew 25:31-46
29. **Shrewd Steward**: Luke 16:1-8
30. **Sowed**: Matthew 13:2-8; 18-23, Mark 4:3-8; 14-20, Luke 8:5-8,11-15
31. **Talents**: Matthew 25:14-30
32. **Tare and Wheat**: Matthew 13:24-30, 36-43
33. **Ten Pounds**: Luke 19:12-27
34. **Ten Virgins**: Matthew 25:1-13
35. **Two Sons**: Matthew 21:28-32
36. **Unfruitful Fig Tree**: Luke 13:6-9
37. **Unmerciful Servant**: Matthew 18:23-35
38. **Watchful Servants**: Mark 13:34-37, Luke 12:35-40
39. **Wedding Banquet**: Matthew 22:2-14
40. **Wise and Foolish Builders:** Matthew 7:24-27, Luke 6:47-49

THE HOLY SPIRIT
MY BELOVED FRIEND

"However when He, the Spirit of truth has come, He will guide you into all truth; for He will not speak on His own authority, but whatever He hears He will speak; and He will tell you things to come. He will glorify Me, for He will take of what is Mine and declare it to you".
"All things that the Father has are Mine. Therefore I said that He will take of Mine and declare it to you."

John 16: 13-15

THE HOLY SPIRIT
MY BELOVED FRIEND

When we think of Jesus Christ, we immediately have a mental picture of a person. Also, when we think of God the Father, we fall heavily on our own preconceptions, but we still may imagine a person.

The Holy Spirit is different. When we think of the Holy Spirit, we have trouble coming up with anything like a mental image of a person. Our imagination is likely to run to something more like a vague fuzzy cloud. Often we think of an invisible impersonal force. No wonder the Holy Spirit is often wrongly referred to as "it". Christians affirm that the Spirit is the third person of the Trinity, which we struggle to think of Him, the Holy Spirit, as a person at all.

The Bible is very clear that the Holy Spirit is a person, yet how can we as human beings truly understand who He is. Scriptures help us by giving us strong word pictures of the Spirit, as a person; yet also scripture gives us visual images as: Wind or Breath, Water, Dove, Fire, Pledge, Counselor, Advocate, Anointing Oil and the Giver of Gifts. So, Jesus does clarify that the Holy Spirit is a person, just as He is a person.

However, when He the Spirit of truth, has come, He will guide you into all truth; for He will not speak on His own authority, but whatever He hears He will speak; and He will tell you things to come. He will glorify Me for He will take of what is Mine and declare to you. All things that the Father has are Mine. Therefore I said that He will take of Mine and declare it to you. (John 16:13-15)

Ask Holy Spirit today to reveal Himself to you and I am sure He will respond to your prayers, as it is important to know Him personally and as a person.

I encourage you to study the scriptures closely. I have outlined some of the pictures and personality of the Holy Spirit and get yourself familiar to our Beloved friend, the Holy Spirit, and He will be there for you.

1. The presence of the Holy Spirit produces the fruit of unconditional love. (Galatians 5:22, Romans 5:5)
2. In a world of falsehood and deceit, the Holy Spirit will give you the ability to discern the spirit and motivation in operation. (1 Corinthians 12:10)

3. Speaking the language of the Holy Spirit exposes one to the secret and hidden truths of God. (1 Corinthians 2:9-10; 14:2)

4. Holy Spirit is the Spirit of Truth; sent to protect, realign and set one free. (John 14:17)

5. Holy Spirit helps one know, recognize and welcome the mind of God, always. (John 14:17)

6. We have friendship with Holy Spirit. Do not promise Holy Spirit, however, what you aren't willing to surrender, for He owns it all. (Acts 5:3-4)

7. Holy Spirit is intense. Avoid whatever suppresses or subdues His flame in your life. (1Thessalonians 5 :19)

8. Intimacy with the Holy Spirit makes Him rise to defend us in the face of the satan's attack. (Isaiah 59:19)

9. Holy Spirit, opens us to receive open visions and heaven from Him. (Joel 2:28, 1 Samuel 3:1)

10. Holy Spirit is allowed in us, therefore He marks us for recognition and blessing. (Joel 2:29)

11. Holy Spirit exposes us to the One who has power to act on behalf of Jesus. (John 14:27)

12. Holy Spirit is here to remind us of all things, physically and spiritually. (John 14:16)

13. Ability to see the past clearly and predict the future becomes possible when building a friendship with the Holy Spirit. (1 Corinthians 12:10)

14. The true understanding of Jesus Christ is only possible as we befriend the Holy Spirit. (John 16:7)

15. Holy Spirit befriends us and continues to remind us of our right standing in God. (John 16:8)

16. Holy Spirit is the embodiment of Truth. As He leads us, we will not fall into error. (John 16:13)

17. Speaking the language of our beloved friend, the Holy Spirit, means we can allow Him to pray through us. (1 Corinthians 14:14, Romans 8:26, Revelation 1:10)

18. Friendship with Holy Spirit leads us to intimacy with the Father forever. (John 16:13)

19. The Spiritual mind-set of heaven is possible, as one walks with the Holy Spirit. (John 16:13)

20. Divine revelation is made possible, as our heavenly Friend keeps us informed. (John 16:13)

21. True worship is possible as the Holy Spirit leads us to the Father's presence. (John 14:14)

22. Holy Spirit gives us access to His wonder working power. (1 Corinthians 12:9)

23. You will not walk in the dark concerning the future. Your Friend is the present and future. (John 16:13)

24. Heavenly manna and purpose come to us from the Father, through the Holy Spirit. (John 16:14)

25. Inheritance in Christ, as the Holy Spirit leads us into full possession. (John16:15)

26. Intimacy with the Holy Spirit frees us from the impact of guilt and condemnation, of our past. (Romans 8:1)

27. My Friend introduces His program and principles to counter what has dominated me. (Romans 8:2)

28. Holy Spirit takes over and helps us live on a higher dimension, forever in Christ Jesus. (Romans 8:4)

29. Friendship with the Holy Spirit and speaking His language, gives us direct access to the Father. (1 Corinthians 2:11; 14:1, 2)

30. The in-dwelling Spirit is the mark of our new life, in Christ Jesus. (Romans 8:9)

31. Holy Spirit dwelling in us brings good health to our physical and spiritual bodies. (Romans 8:1)

32. Intimacy with the Holy Spirit means starvation for the carnal nature in us. (Romans 8:13)

33. By saying yes to Him and the things He desires, lifts us to the position of mature sons. (Romans 8:14)

34. When the Holy Spirit prays through us, in His language, He bypasses our human understanding. (I Corinthians 14:14; James 1:8)

35. Freedom from all bondages is made possible through the Holy Spirit. (Romans 8:15a)

36. Holy Spirit is God's solution to our need for perpetual counseling. (John14:16, Jeremiah 32:19)

37. The Fatherhood of God is grasped through the inspiration of Holy Spirit. (Romans 8:15b,16)

38. In-dwelling of the Holy Spirit in us, is a token of future, blissful living. (Romans 8:23)

39. Your limitations become insignificant in the presence of the Holy Spirit. (Romans 8:26)

40. Intercession can be reached through the help of the Holy Spirit in us. (Romans 8:26b, Jude: 20)

41. Walking and living in the Spirit is the answer to living according to His dominion. (Galatians 5:16)

42. Friendship with the Holy Spirit guarantees the presence of His fruitful qualities. (Galatians 5:22)

43. The presence of the Holy Spirit produces the fruit of unconditional love. (Romans 5:5, Galatians 5:22)

44. He brings the capacity for gladness of heart that is not produced by temporal goods. (Galatians 5:22)

45. Holy Spirit brings tranquility, beyond human comprehension. (Galatians 5:22, Philippians 4:7)

46. The in-dwelling Holy Spirit is the answer to handling the pressures of this world. (Galatians 5:22)

47. Holy Spirit *opens* us to overflowing, with the milk of kindness. (Galatians 5:22)

48. Holy Spirit will touch others through us, as we walk and show compassion. (Galatians 5:22)

49. Holy Spirit gives us the ability to stay true and committed to the purposes of God. (Galatians 5:22)

50. Holy Spirit is the only One that produces meekness and temperance without measure in our lives. (Galatians 5:23)

51. Holy Spirit produces the ability to walk in Self-restraint and constraint. (Galatians 5:23)

52. Relationship with the Holy Spirit elevates us to operate in supernatural knowledge of the past, present and future. (1 Corinthians 12:8)

53. Divine understanding in impossible situations and the wisdom to bring solutions, is a gift of the Holy Spirit. (1 Corinthians 12:8, Job 32:8)

54. Through the Holy Spirit, we can move in the gift of miracles. (1 Corinthians 12:10)

55. Friendship with the Holy Spirit means He is able to refresh and renew us in moments of physical and spiritual burnout. (Romans 8:27, Isaiah 28:12)

56. Holy Spirit is the key to fully surrendering our tongue. (Ephesians 4:29; 5:4, Isaiah 30:15)

57. The Holy Spirit and speaking His language, shuts out worldly pressures. (1 John. 2:15)

58. Praying in the language of Holy Spirit helps avoid doubt in what we ask, while praying. (Mark 11:23, I Corinthians 14:15)

59. The Holy Spirit fills us, when the human spirit fails. (Acts 4:8)

60. The Holy Spirit overshadows and gives divine ability, efficiency and might. (Acts 1:8)

61. The in-dwelling Holy Spirit in us, is the mark of God's approval. (Ephesians 4:30)

62. The in-dwelling Holy Spirit in us, is the indication of our inheritance. (Ephesians 1:14)

63. Holy Spirit requires that we avoid whatever offends, vexes or saddens Him. (Ephesians 4:30)

64. Friendship with Holy Spirit protects us from being frivolous with words. (Job 32:18)

65. Friendship with Holy Spirit makes available, the seven Spirits of the Lord: to rest upon us, wisdom, understanding, counsel, might, knowledge and fear of the Lord. (Isaiah 11:2)

66. Holy Spirit is the only Friend who can be with us everywhere, at all times. (Psalm 139:7-10)

67. Speaking the language of Holy Spirit results in our spirit being built up. (1 Corinthians 14:4, Jude: 20)

68. Friendship with Holy Spirit exposes our minds to wisdom and creativity. (Exodus 31:3; 35:31)

69. Friendship with Holy Spirit results in our being led into that which is right. (Psalm 143:10)

70. Holy Spirit empowers us to proclaim God's Word. (Isaiah 61:1)

71. Holy Spirit fills us with the desire to help the meek, the afflicted and the brokenhearted. (Isaiah 61:1)

72. Holy Spirit gets in-depth with us as we speak the language He gives us. (1 Corinthians 12:10, Jude 1:20)

73. Relationship with Him makes available His presence and power without measure. (John 3:34)

74. Relationship with Him makes available the yoke destroying and burden removing power of God. (John 3:34)

75. As we commune with Him, Holy Spirit is capable of lifting and taking us to new heights, like never before. (Ezekiel 3:14)

76. Holy Spirit gives us keys to operating with excellence, in the spiritual realm. (Daniel 5:12; 6:3)

77. The Holy Spirit is our ever present help, in time of need. (John 14:16, Psalms 46:1)

78. Holy Spirit strengthens, so we can move and do things in His power. (Luke 4:14)

79. Holy Spirit will supply a continuous dosage of spiritual zeal for you. (Acts 18:25)

80. Friendship with the Holy Spirit gives divine wisdom, understanding, counsel, might, knowledge and of the fear of the LORD. (Isaiah 11:2)

81. Friendship with Him makes hidden things that are beyond human understanding made available through insight. (Daniel 4:8)

82. Intimacy with Holy Spirit transforms us from the spirit of fear to the spirit of boldness. (2 Timothy 1:7)

83. The Holy Spirit is also of the future, so His language is best for giving God the highest praise. (1 Corinthians 14:15, Ephesians 5:19)

84. Presence of the Holy Spirit makes us God's hallowed, special residence. (1 Corinthians 6:11)

85. His presence in us provokes satan's abuse, but we are blessed and highly favored. (Acts 7:55)

86. The in-dwelling of the Holy Spirit brings favor we do not deserve. (Zechariah. 12:10)

87. Friendship with the Holy Spirit produces supernatural knowledge. (Isaiah 11:2)

88. Holy Spirit is the best defense counsel, to argue our case. (Isaiah. 4:5,16, Psalms 94:22)

89. Holy Spirit is our perpetual intercessor, always praying for us. (John14:16, Romans 8:27, Psalms 139:1-2)

90. One purpose of Holy Spirit coming is to befriend us. (John 14:16)

91. Openness in our relationship with Him, makes extraordinary power available, to minister divine healing. (1 Corinthians 12:9)

92. Holy Spirit enables. Divine energy is ours because of your fellowship with Him. (John 14:16)

93. Holy Spirit is ready to respond, in all major and minor challenges of our lives. (John 14:16)

94. Spiritual birth is possible when it is orchestrated and conducted through the Holy Spirit. (John 3:5)

95. Friendship with Holy Spirit is the basis for true, deep and genuine worship. (John 4:23, 24)

96. Holy Spirit becomes a well of living, satisfying water; quenching our spiritual thirst. (John 14:14)

97. He makes His presence go beyond a well of truth, to become the rivers of living water. (John 7:37)

98. The Holy Spirit has a beautiful language that He not only wants to speak, but sing through us. (1 Corinthians 14:15, Ephesians. 5:19)

99. Friendship with the Holy Spirit helps keep our visions and dreams alive. (Joel 2:28)

100. The in-dwelling presence of the Holy Spirit makes perpetual power available to us. (Ephesians 3:20)

101. Friendship with the Holy Spirit produces reverence and obedient fear of the Lord. (Isaiah 11:2)

102. Holy Spirit helps during the time of our weakness. (Romans 8:26)

103. Holy Spirit is our Advocate and attorney general. (Romans 8: 22-25)

104. Holy Spirit empowers us in our weakness or insufficiency while praying. (Romans 8:26)

105. Holy Spirit conveys the Spirit's exertion and earnestness, in prayer for us. (Romans 8:26)

106. Holy Spirit aligned your Spirit's prayers with what God wants for you. (Romans 8:27)

107. Through His power, Holy Spirit enables us to minister in a unique or particular way. (1 Corinthians 12: 1-11)

108. Friendship with Him moves us to higher levels of maturity in Christ Jesus. (Acts.13:6-13)

109. Friendship with Holy Spirit will showcase, teach and confirm His zeal in us. (1 Corinthians 2:13, Acts 13:1-5)

110. As we befriend the Holy Spirit, He protects us from calamity. (Numbers. 24:2)

111. As we befriend the Holy Spirit, He often reveals Himself as: a man, water, fire, wind or breath, anointing oil, pledge, counselor, advocate, dove, and the giver of gifts. (Isaiah. 11:2)

THE POWER IN THE NAME OF OUR LORD JESUS CHRIST

LORD JESUS CHRIST, is the most powerful and anointed Name in heaven, on earth and below. In this prayer book, I have listed most of these Names for you to call upon and examine during times of challenge. By calling this dynamite Name, the rocks and mountains of life will surely melt.

- *"In the name of **Jesus Christ** of Nazareth, rise up and walk."* (Acts 3:6)
- *"Let it be known to you all, and to all the people of Israel, that by the name of **Jesus Christ** of Nazareth, whom you crucified, who God raised from the dead, by Him this man stands here before you whole."* (Acts 4:10)
- *"Men who have risked their lives for the name of our **Lord Jesus Christ**."* (Acts 15:26)
- *"Now I plead with you, brethren, by the name of our **Lord Jesus Christ**, that you all speak the same thing, and*

that there be no divisions among you, but that you be perfectly joined together in the same mind and in the same judgment." (1 Corinthians 1:10)

- *"For whoever calls on the name of that Lord shall be saved." (Romans. 10:13)*
- *In the name of our **Lord Jesus Christ**, when you are gathered together, along with my spirit, with the power of our Lord Jesus Christ."* (1 Corinthians 5:4)
- *"Giving thanks always for all things to God the Father in the name of our **Lord Jesus Christ**."* (Ephesians 5:20)
- *"That the name of our Lord Jesus Christ may be glorified in you, and you in Him, according to the grace of our God and **the Lord Jesus Christ**."* (2 Thessalonians 1:12)
- *"But we command you, brethren, in the name of our **Lord Jesus Christ**, that you withdraw from every brother who walks disorderly and not according to the tradition which he received from us."* (2 Thessalonians 3:6)

When we call on the wonderful Name of Jesus Christ, daily, in our prayers and meditate on His name; immediately, the supernatural happens in our lives, whether we know it or not.

This is the name the Almighty Father reckoned with and this is the name the Holy Spirit Himself can hear, speak and declare to you. It is a great privilege for us to study and be acquainted with this distinguished and marvelous name, of our Lord Jesus Christ. The bible tells us many things about this wonderful name. (Isaiah 9:6)

Remember, the Name of Jesus Christ is power, so when you call upon His Name, it is a prayer. By simply calling His Name, you can be healed from all illnesses, delivered from evils and be closer to Him. Start calling this wonderful and marvelous Name today, aloud in your house, car, anywhere you can open your mouth. You'll see how He shows up supernaturally, to address your situations.

This is the only Name that can be called upon as a prescription. His name will fix all things in heaven, on earth and below. The Name of Jesus is power.

1. Adam (1 Corinthians 15:45)
2. Advocate (1 John 2:1)
3. Almighty (Revelation 1:8)
4. Alpha and Omega (Revelation 1:8)
5. Amen (Revelation 3:14)
6. Apostle of our Profession (Hebrews 3:1)
7. Arm of the Lord (Isaiah 51:9; 53:1)
8. Author and Finisher of Our Faith (Hebrews 12:2)
9. Author of Eternal Salvation (Hebrews 5:9)
10. Beginning of Creation of God (Revelation 3:14)
11. Beloved Son (Matthew 12:18)
12. Blessed and Only Potentate (1 Timothy 6:15)

13. Branch (Isaiah 4:2)
14. BRANCH (Zechariah 6:12)
15. Bread of Life (John 6:32)
16. Breath of the Almighty (Job 32:8; 33:4)
17. Bridegroom (Matthew 9:15)
18. Brother of James, Joseph, Judas, and Simon (Mark 6:3)
19. Captain of Salvation (Hebrews 2:10)
20. Carpenter's son (Matthew 6:3)
21. Chief Shepherd (1 Peter 5:4)
22. Chief Cornerstone, elect and precious (1 Peter 2:6)
23. Christ of God (Luke 9:20)
24. Consolation of Israel (Luke 2:25)
25. Cornerstone (Psalm 118:22)
26. Counselor (Isaiah 9:6)
27. Creator (John 1:3)
28. Dayspring (Luke 1:78)
29. Deliverer (Romans 11:26)
30. Desire of Nations (Haggai 2:7)
31. Door (John 10:7)
32. Elect of God (Isaiah 42:1)
33. Everlasting Father (Isaiah 9:6)
34. Faithful Witness (Revelation 1:5)
35. First and Last (Revelation 1:17)
36. First Begotten Son (Revelation 1:5)
37. Forerunner (Hebrews 6:20)
38. Fountain of Living Waters (Jeremiah 2:13)
39. Glory of the LORD (Isaiah 40:5)
40. God (Isaiah 40:3)
41. God Blessed (Romans 9:5)
42. Good Shepherd (John 10:11)

43. Governor (Matthew 2:6)
44. Great High Priest (Hebrews 4:14)
45. Head of Church (Ephesians 1:22)
46. Heir of all Things (Hebrews 1:2)
47. Holy Child (Acts 4:27)
48. Holy One (Acts 3:14)
49. Holy One of God (Mark 1:24)
50. Holy One of Israel (Isaiah 41:14)
51. Horn of Salvation (Luke 1:69)
52. I AM (John 8:58)
53. Image of God (2 Corinthians 4:4)
54. Immanuel (Isaiah 7:14)
55. Intercessor (Isaiah 53:12)
56. Jehovah (Isaiah 26:4)
57. JESUS (Matthew 1:21)
58. Jesus Christ (John 1:17, Acts 2:38)
59. Jesus of Nazareth (Matthew 21:11)
60. Jesus Christ our Lord (Romans 1:3)
61. Jesus Christ our Savior (Titus 3:6)
62. Judge of the righteous (2 Timothy 4:8)
63. Judge of Israel (Micah 5:1)
64. Just One (Acts 7:52)
65. King (Zechariah 9:9)
66. King of Ages (1 Timothy 1:17)
67. King of Jews (Matthew 2:2)
68. King of Kings (1 Timothy 6:15)
69. King of Saints (Revelation 15:3)
70. Lawgiver (Isaiah 33:22)
71. Lamb (Revelation 13)
72. Lamb of God (John 1:29)
73. Leader and Commander (Isaiah 55:4)

74. Life (John 14:6)
75. Light of life (John 8:12)
76. Light of the World (John 8:12)
77. Lion of Tribe of Judah (Revelation 5:5)
78. Lord of All (Acts 10:36)
79. Lord of Glory (1 Corinthians 2:8)
80. Lord of Lords (1 Timothy 6:15)
81. Lord of our Righteousness (Jeremiah 23:6)
82. Man of Sorrows (Isaiah 53:3)
83. Mediator (1 Timothy 2:5)
84. Messenger of Covenant (Malachi 3:1)
85. Messiah (Daniel 9:25, John 1:41)
86. Mighty God (Isaiah 9:6)
87. Mighty One (Isaiah 60:16)
88. Morning Star (Revelation 22:16)
89. Nazarene (Matthew 2:23)
90. Only Begotten Son (John 1:18)
91. Our Passover (1 Corinthians 5:7)
92. Prince of Life (Acts 3:15)
93. Prince of Kings (Revelation 1:5)
94. Prince of Peace (Isaiah 9:6)
95. Prophet (Luke 24:19, Acts 3:22)
96. Redeemer (Job 19:25)
97. Resurrection and Life (John 11:25)
98. Rock (1 Corinthians 10:4)
99. Root of David (Revelation 22:16)
100. Rose of Sharon (Song of Songs 2:1)
101. Savior (Luke 2:11)
102. Seed of Woman (Genesis 3:15)
103. Shepherd and Bishop of Souls (1 Peter 2:25)
104. Shiloh (Genesis 49:10)

105. Shiloh of Blessed (Mark 14:61)
106. Son of David (Matthew 1:1)
107. Son of God (Matthew 2:15)
108. Son of Highest (Luke 1:32)
109. Sun of Righteousness (Malachi 4:2)
110. True Light (John 1:9)
111. True Vine (John 15:1)
112. Truth (John 1:14)
113. Witness (Isaiah 55:4)
114. Word (John 1:1)
115. Word of God (Revelation 19:13)

SPIRITUAL AND BIBLICAL SIGNIFICANCE OF NUMBERS

By using this daily devotional prayer book I do believe God will speak and reveal things more often than you may have ever experienced before. One way God communicates with us is through numbers. Numbers are highly symbolic in the Bible as well as in prophetic dreams and great care must be exercised in properly interpreting their meaning. Here are few basic principles for interpreting symbolic numbers that will help prevent error. We outlined number one through thirteen.

1. The simple numbers of 1-13 often have spiritual significance.

2. Multiples of these numbers, or doubling or tripling carrying basically the same meaning, only they intensify the truth. The number 100, for example, would have the same meaning as the number ten, but greatly magnified.

3. The first use of the number in Scripture generally conveys its spiritual meaning.

4. Numbers should be interpreted consistently throughout Scripture, as God is consistent.

5. The spiritual significance is not always stated, but may be veiled, hidden, or seen in comparison with other Scripture.

6. Generally, there is good and evil; true and counterfeit; and godly and satanic; aspects of numbers.

With these six principles above, let's consider the symbolic meaning of individual numbers.

ONE - God, Beginning, Source: The number of Wholeness and Unity

In the beginning, God who is One created the heavens and earth. (Genesis 1:1)

But seek first (number one priority) His kingdom and His righteousness, and all these things will be added to you. (Matthew 6:33)

- **Day One Creation**: Light was created.
- One excludes all differences.
- "One Lord, One Faith, One Baptism." (Ephesians 4:5)
- One represents the universal, whole and complete.

- "Hear, O Israel; the LORD our God, the LORD is One." (Deuteronomy 6:4)
- One represents God as the beginning and the end, the prime impulse and the source of creation.
- One usually represents God, His sovereign rule, His omnipotence, His supremacy and His unique character.
- One also represents harmony, unity or peace because of its reference to God.
- One is independent of all other numbers and is the source of all other numbers.

TWO – Witness, Testimony: The number of Covenant, Mutuality and Accord

"On the evidence of two witnesses or three witnesses, he who is to die shall put to death; he shall not be put to death on the evidence of one witness." (Deuteronomy 17:6).

"Even in your law it has been written that the testimony of two men is true." (John 8:17)

- **Day-Two Creation**: Heaven above and Water below were created.
- The Son has two natures: human and divine
- There are two types of people: sheep and goats.
- The first time that the word two is used in the bible is in relation to this theme of division.

- There are two ages; this age and the age to come. (Matthew 12:32; 13:39, 40, 49, Mark 10:30)
- There are two testaments; the Old and New. Man is male and female, marriage and partnership.
- Romans 9 speaks of two vessels. One vessel for honorable use and the other for dishonorable use.
- Two is unity plus another, thus we have a difference or contrast between the one and the other.
- Two can also represent solemn agreement, legal bonding and mutual promises of God.
- Two is the first number by which we can divide another. In all of its uses, this fundamental idea of division or difference is evident.
- The sun and the moon were to mark out the division between day and night.

THREE - Godhead, Divine Completeness: The Indivisible Power

"Go therefore and make disciples of all the nations, baptizing them in name of Father and the Son and the Holy Spirit (three-in-one), teaching them to observe all that I commanded you; and lo, I am with you always, even to the end of the age." (Matthew 28:19-20)

- **Day Three Creation**: Earth, Sea, and Vegetation were created.

- Three represents Divine perfection.
- Three represents the number of invincibility.
- The Trinity consists of Father, Son, and the Holy Spirit.
- The three divisions of time: past, present and future.
- God's three main attributes: Omnipotence, Omnipresence and Omniscience (Revelations 19:6)

FOUR – Earth, Creation, Winds, Seasons: The number of Divine Creation

"All flesh is not the same flesh, but there is one flesh of men, and another flesh of beasts, and another flesh of birds, and another of fish." (four kinds of flesh in creation) (1 Corinthians 15:39)

Then He said to me, "Prophesy to the breath, prophesy son of man, and say to the breath," Thus says the Lord God, "Come from the four winds, O breath, and breathe on these slain, that they come to life." (Ezekiel 37:9)

- **Day Four Creation**: Sun, Moon, and Stars were created.
- Four corners of the earth (**north, south, east and west)**
- The four seasons. (spring, summer, autumn and winter)
- The materials of the tabernacle were four and so were the coverings and the ornamentations.
- The fourth commandment is the first commandment that refers to the earth and the fourth clause of the Lord's Prayer is the first that mentions the earth.

- *Against Elam I will bring the four winds from the four quarters of heaven and scatter them toward all those winds where the outcasts of Elam will not go.* (Jeremiah 49:36)
- *The hands of a man were under their wings on their four sides; and each of the four had faces and wings.* (Ezekiel 1:8)
- Other scriptures with the number four: Daniel 7:6, Zechariah 6:5, Acts 10:11
- "And a river went out of Eden to water the garden; and from thence it was parted, and became into four heads." (Genesis 2:10)
- King replied, "Look!" he answered, "I see four men loose walking in the midst of the fire; and they are not hurt, and the form of the fourth is like the Son of God." (Daniel 3:24-28)

FIVE – Cross, Grace, Atonement: The Number of Grace

- **Day Five Creation**: Living Creatures of Water and Sky were created.
- David picked up five smooth stones to fight Goliath. (1 Samuel 17:40)
- The five-fold offices of ministry: apostle, prophet, evangelist, pastor and teacher. (Ephesians 4:11-13)

- The Holy Anointing Oil was pure and composed of five ingredients. (Exodus 30:23-25)
- The five gifts of God to humankind: Christianity, infinite love, mercy, favor, and goodwill shown to humankind, by God.

SIX – Manifestation of Man, Beast, Satan: The number of flesh and humanity

- **Day Six Creation**: Living creatures on land and humans were created.
- Man was created on the 6th day. (Genesis 1:24-31)
- Man labors six days of the week.
- The serpent was created on the 6th day. (Genesis 1:24-31)
- The sixth commandment is "Thou shall not murder." (Genesis 20:13)
- Six is clearly stamped in the bible as the number of man. (Genesis 1:26)
- Six words are used for man: Adam, ISH, ENOSH, GEHVER, ANTHROPPOS, ANAR.
- The number of the beast in Revelation is 666. (Revelation 13:18)
- The number of the antichrist 6 x 6 = 36.
- Note that when adding (36 + 35 + 34 + 33 + 32 ...5 + 4 + 3 + 2 +1)= 666

SEVEN – Perfection, Completeness. The number Divine Revolutions and Cycles.

- God completed His creative work on the seventh day and rested (Genesis 2:1-2).
- In the book of Joshua, the Israelites marched around Jericho once a day for six days and on the seventh day, they marched seven times. When their march was completed, they blew trumpets and shouted and the walls of Jericho fell. (Joshua 6:1-27).
- **Day Seven Creation**: Rest was established by the Creator.
- Seven of the Ten Commandments begin with the Word **"Not."**
- Seven colors in the color spectrum.
- Seven parables in the book of Matthew and Seven promises to the churches.
- Book of Revelations revealed seven of each: angels, plagues, candlesticks, seals, churches, spirit, heads, thunders, horns, thunders of creation, mountains, trumpets, vials and lamps.
- **Seven "Eternals" in the book of Hebrews**:
    1) Priest for Ever (Hebrews1:6)
    2) Eternal Salvation (Hebrews 1:9)
    3) Eternal Judgment (Hebrews 6:2)
    4) Eternal Redemption (Hebrews 9:12)

5) Eternal Spirit (Hebrews 9:14)

6) Eternal Inheritance (Hebrews 9:15)

7) Everlasting Covenant (Hebrews 13:20).

- **Seven Things Jesus said on the cross:**

    1. Jesus said, "Father, forgive them, for they do not know what they are doing." (Luke 23:34)

    2. Jesus answered him, "I tell you the truth, today you will be with me in paradise." (Luke 23:43)

    3. About the ninth hour Jesus cried out in a loud voice, "Eloi, Eloi, lama sabachthani." (Matt 27:46)

    4. When Jesus saw his mother there, and the disciple whom he loved standing nearby, he said to his mother, "Dear woman, here is your son." (John 19:26)

    5. Later, knowing that all was now completed, and so that the Scripture would be fulfilled, Jesus said, "I am thirsty." (John 19:28)

    6. When he had received the drink, Jesus said, "It is finished." (John19:30)

    7. Jesus called out with a loud voice, "Father, into your hands I commit my spirit." (Luke 23:46)

EIGHT – The Number of New Beginnings

As a sign of God's covenant with Israel, every male was to be circumcised when he was eight days old. (Genesis17:10-12)

When the Lord sent a great flood on the earth, He saved eight people, Noah and his family, in an ark to make a new beginning (1 Peter 3:20).

Many agree that the modern prophetic movement had its origins in 1988. This was birthing time of new beginning for the Body of Christ.

- It signals the beginning of a new era.
- God made eight covenants with Abraham
- Circumcision is done on eighth day. (Genesis 17:12)
- Eight people were saved in the Ark. (2 Peter 2:5).
- Eight represents regeneration and resurrection.
- David was Jesse's eighth son, who coincidentally marked the new monarchical reign of Israel after Saul. (1Samuel 16:7-13)
- Eight souls were saved from the antediluvian flood, through water on Noah's Ark. (1 Peter 3:18-20)
- Eight is seven plus one: perfection plus unity, and is hence the start of a new order.

NINE – Finality, Fullness. The Number of Gestation, Reproduction, Maturity, Development, Judgment and Deliverance.

- There are nine **Gifts of the Spirit**: word of wisdom, the word of knowledge, faith, healing, miracles, prophecy, discerning of spirits, tongues and interpretation of tongues. (1 Cor.12:8-10)

- There are nine **Fruits of the Spirit:** love, joy, peace, patience, kindness, goodness, faithfulness, gentleness and self control. (Galatians 5:22-23)

- Dan means a judge. The number nine represents finality or judgment.

- Nine Lepers, are they not ten; One came back to thank Jesus, the other nine lepers did not come back. (Luke: 17:11-19)

- Nine is not yet full or complete, like the number ten, yet does mark the ending of single digit numbers. Thus, nine can represent the conclusion or ending of a matter/ period.

- Woman when pregnant, usually carry the baby for nine months and then delivers.

- There are Nine Greek words derived from the root word meaning judgment (dikay). These words each occur nine times in scripture.

  o Abussos (**bottomless pit**)

○ Asebee (**ungodly**)

○ Aselgeia (**lasciviousness**)

○ Astrapee (**lightning**)

TEN – Law and Government: The number of the Creator, God's divine law and divine perfection.

- There were ten plagues placed on Egypt. (Exodus 9:14)
- The 10 x 10 silver sockets formed the foundation of the Tabernacle. (Exodus 38:27)
- The tithe is 1/10 of your income. Ten is the number of divine economy and diverse elements of it.
- Ten was declared in the bible (ten commandments, ten plagues, ten lepers, ten virgins, ten requests of Daniel)
- There are ten commandments, which are the laws of God for humanity (Exodus 20:1-end, 34:28, Deuteronomy 4:13; 10:4)
- There are ten "I AM's" spoken by Jesus Christ in the book of John.
  1. *I am the Bread of Life.* (6:35)
  2. *I am the Bread of Life which came down from heaven.* (6:41)
  3. *I am the Living Bread.* (6:51)
  4. *I am the Light of the world.* (8:12)
  5. *I am One who bears witness of Myself.* (8:18)
  6. *I am the Door of the sheep.* (10:7, 9)

7. I am the Good Shepherd. (10:14)

8. I am the Resurrection and the Life. (11:25)

9. I am the Way, the Truth, and the Life. (14:6)

10. I am the True Vine. (15:1, 5)

ELEVEN – Disorganization, Lawlessness, Antichrist: The number of revelation and True Witness.

*As for the ten horns, out of this kingdom ten kings will arise; and another (**the eleventh**) will arise after them and he will be different from the previous ones and will subdue three kings. He will speak out against the Most High and wear down the saints of the Highest One, and he will intend to make alterations in times and in law; and they will be given into his hand for a time, times and half a time. But the court will sit for the judgment and his dominion will be taken away, annihilated and destroyed forever.* (Daniel 7:24)

- The number of disorder and judgment.
- Then eleven is perfect organization plus one more, one extra.
- Joseph was the eleventh son of Jacob. (Genesis 49:22-26)
- Jacob took his eleven sons to see his brothers. (Genesis 32:22)

- One more than required, an extra measure, something more than only what is required.
- The number of paradigm shifts; eleven is a transitional number and divine injunction of government. (Acts 1:26)
- Jesus finds his disciples at the eleventh hour standing idle. (Matthew 20:6-9)
- Jesus appeared to His disciples eleven times in the bible.
- Then the eleven disciples went away into Galilee, to the mountain which Jesus had appointed for them. (Matthew 28:16)
- The parting of the Red sea is the eleventh plague God used against Egypt. *Then the waters returned and covered the chariots, the horsemen, and all the army of Pharaoh that came into the sea after them. Not so much as one of them remained.* (Exodus 14:28)

TWELVE – Divine Government, Apostolic fullness: The number of Divine Government and Apostolic Rule
- There were twelve tribes of Israel (Exodus 28:21)
- Jesus chose twelve disciples. (Matthew 10:2-4)
- The number of divine government and apostolic rule
- Twelve is the number of God's covenanted ones in power and authority

- Twelve is the number of the rule of God's covenanted ones, particularly His apostles (1 Kings 9:29, Jeremiah 1:3; 39:2-3, Matthew 19:28, Revelation 21:12-14).
- Twelve represents the consummate divine and human ruler-ship under Creator God.
- Twelve **wells of water** with **seventy palm trees** were found by the Israelis in Elim, and they camped there by the water. (Exodus 15:27)
- The number twelve represents the epitome of consummate divine and human ruler-ship under Creator God.
- Twelve is one of the perfect numbers. Three is divine perfection. Seven is spiritual perfection. Ten is ordinal perfection and twelve is governmental perfection.
- There are twelve tribes of Israel, twelve apostles and twelve disciples of Christ. There are twelve foundations in the heavenly Jerusalem: twelve gates, twelve pearls, twelve angels. The measurements of the New Jerusalem are 12,000 furlongs, while the wall will be 144 (or 12 x 12). (Revelation 21:16-17)

THIRTEEN – Rebellion, Backsliding, Apostasy

Twelve years they had served Chedorlaomer, but the ***thirteenth year*** *they rebelled"* (Genesis 14:4).

This is the first appearance in Scripture of the number 13, which sets the standard for its interpretation.

- Rebellion
- Matthias is the thirteenth of the Apostles.

DAILY SCRIPTURE REFERENCE

Our journey in life differs each day as we walk together, in Christ Jesus. The subjects listed below will help you quickly to delve into the scriptures and get soaked in the Word of God while you are in that particular place in which you need the "Word" most, to confront that situation.

"This Book of the Law shall not depart from your mouth, but you shall meditate in it day and night, that you may observe to do according to all that is written in it. For then you will make your way prosperous, and then you will have good success. Have I not command you? Be strong and of good courage; do not be afraid, nor be dismayed, for the LORD you God is with you wherever you go" (Joshua 1:8-9)

1. Ability to love (Psalms 116)
2. Adoration (Ezekiel 43)

3. Adoration (Galatians 4)
4. Adoration (Mark 11)
5. Advent (Isaiah 9)
6. Approaching God (Exodus 34)
7. Ascension (Acts 1)
8. Awakening (Psalms 147)
9. Be Filled with Grace (1Timothy 1)
10. Be used by God (Psalms 138)
11. Becoming like Christ (Romans 12)
12. Before a meal (Proverb 13)
13. Before Holy Communion (John1)
14. Benediction (Exodus 19)
15. Benediction (Leviticus 19)
16. Celebrating God (Joshua 24)
17. Children of God (1 Chronicles 4
18. Children of God (2 Chronicles 1)
19. Cleansing (Joshua 7)
20. Comfort (Lamentations 3)
21. Confession (Ezra 10)
22. Confession (Leviticus 16)
23. Confession (Psalms 51)
24. Contentment (Acts 26)
25. Courage (Deuteronomy 31, Joshua 1, Joshua 10)
26. Dependency (Habakkuk 2)
27. Direction (Proverb 3)
28. Discernment (Jeremiah 8)
29. Divine light (Micah 7)
30. Effective ministry (2 Corinthians 12)
31. Encouraging spirit (Proverb 16)
32. Enjoyment of creation (Genesis 2)
33. Experience joy (Psalms 65)

34. Faith (Isaiah 65)
35. Fervor of the soul (Ecclesiastes 8)
36. Forgiveness (Number 21)
37. Fulfillment of God's Will (Genesis 39)
38. God's blessing (Deuteronomy 24)
39. God's blessing (Number 6)
40. God's comfort (Jeremiah 31)
41. God's greatness (Job 37)
42. God's mercy (1 Samuel 7)
43. God's servants (Daniel 3)
44. God's strength (Jonah 2)
45. God's tender care (1 Chronicles 11)
46. God's tender care (2 Chronicles 14)
47. God's truth (Nehemiah 13)
48. Good Friday (Luke 23)
49. Gratitude (Genesis 9)
50. Gratitude for God's Invitation (Luke 5)
51. Greater love (Song of Songs 8)
52. Guidance (Deuteronomy 30)
53. Guidance (Job 12)
54. Guidance (John 14)
55. Holy living (Malachi 2)
56. Holy Spirit (Acts 2)
57. Holy Spirit manifestations (Titus 3)
58. Hope (1 Thessalonians 4)
59. Hungering after God (Psalms 27)
60. Illumination and adoration (Revelation 1 and Revelation 11)
61. Indwelling of the Spirit (1 Kings 8)
62. Intercession for leaders (Exodus 3)
63. Knowledge of God (Job 28)

64. Life eternal (1 John 5)
65. Lifelong direction (Zachariah 10)
66. Live for God (Philippians 1)
67. Longing and Trust (Acts 9 and Acts 16)
68. Love (Song of Songs 2)
69. Love of God (Leviticus 25)
70. Loving Others (Colossians 2)
71. Mercy (Jeremiah 15)
72. Mercy (Luke 18)
73. Mercy and knowledge (Hosea 6)
74. Mind of God (Exodus 25)
75. Morning (Psalms 5)
76. Morning prayers (Psalms 92)
77. Obedience (Matthew 16)
78. Offering petitions (Genesis 18)
79. Oppressed (Judges 3)
80. Oppressed (Proverb 29)
81. Our Creator (Psalms 8)
82. Our departure from this world (2 Kings 2)
83. Our enemies (Matthew 5)
84. Our pilgrimage (Amos 5)
85. Pardon (Samuel 1)
86. Parents for their Children (Luke 8)
87. Peace (1 Samuel 30)
88. Perseverance (Number 33)
89. Perseverance and Remembrance of the Saints (Hebrews 10 and 12)
90. Poor and oppressed (Isaiah 25)
91. Praise for the Resurrection (Matthew 27)
92. Praise for the Resurrection (Matthew 28)
93. Protection (Exodus 14)

94. Pure Conscience (Leviticus 6)
95. Refreshment (1 Kings 17)
96. Refreshment (1 Kings 22)
97. Refreshment (1 Samuel 1)
98. Release from bondage (Ezekiel 11)
99. Release from fear (Esther 4)
100. Remembrance (Deuteronomy 9)
101. Renewal (2 Kings 12)
102. Renewal (Ezra 1)
103. Renewed understanding (Isaiah 55)
104. Repentance (Zephaniah 2)
105. Resisting temptation (Genesis 4)
106. Returning to God's Presence (Jeremiah 50)
107. Righteous King (Jeremiah 23)
108. Run the Race before Us (2 Timothy 4)
109. Sanctification and a Loving Heart (1 Corinthians 4, 13)
110. Scattered and Lost (Ruth2)
111. Seeking God First (Mark 8)
112. Self-abandonment (Job 1)
113. Self-Control (Number 3)
114. Serving God (Romans 6)
115. Share in Christ's Sufferings (Matthew 20)
116. Sharing in Christ's Sufferings (John 19)
117. Showing God's Love (1 Samuel 1)
118. Sleep (Mark 4)
119. Social compassion (Isaiah 3)
120. Spirit of Peace (1 Peter 5)
121. Spiritual Armor (Ephesians 6)
122. Steadfast heart (Joshua 12)
123. Steadfastness (Genesis 22)

124. Taking Up Our Cross (Luke 14)
125. Thanksgiving (1 Chronicles 17)
126. Thanksgiving (2 Chronicles 31)
127. Thanksgiving (Joel 2)
128. Thanksgiving (Psalms 19)
129. Those we have neglected (Matthew 25)
130. Those who are weary (1 Samuel 21)
131. Those who mourn (Samuel 1)
132. Time of sickness (2 Kings 20)
133. Times of persecution (Nehemiah 4)
134. Transforming the past (Judges 16)
135. Trials (Matthew 10)
136. Understanding of God's Word (Deuteronomy 8)
137. Understanding our value to God (Isaiah 43)
138. Watchfulness (Daniel 12)
139. Weariness and cynicism (Ecclesiastes 2)
140. Wisdom (1 Kings 3)
141. Work of the Church (Luke 1)
142. Worship (Genesis 32)
143. Worship for Christ Our Mediator (Hebrews 2)
144. Worshipping God (James 5)

Holy Spirit Manufactured Prayer

After these things I looked, and behold, a great multitude
which no one could number, of all *nations, tribes, peoples,
and tongues,* standing before the throne and before the
Lamb, clothed with *white robes*, with *palm branches* in their
hands, and crying out with a loud voice, saying,
**"Salvation belongs to our God who sits on the throne,
and to the Lamb!"**
All the angles stood around the throne and the elders and
the four living creatures, and fell on their faces before the
throne and worshipped God,
Saying:
"Amen! Blessing and glory and wisdom
Thanksgiving and honor and
power and might,
Be to our God forever and ever.
Amen."

Revelation 7:9-12

Holy Spirit Manufactured Prayer

"He who has an ear, let him hear what the Spirit says to the churches. To him who overcomes I will give some of the hidden manna to eat. And I will give him a white stone, and on the stone a new name written which no one knows except him who receives it."

Revelation 2:17

CPSIA information can be obtained at www.ICGtesting.com
Printed in the USA
LVOW120942230312

274464LV00001B/10/P